JAMES STOKES LECTURESHIP
ON POLITICS
NEW YORK UNIVERSITY
(STOKES FOUNDATION)

HUMAN RIGHTS IN THE MODERN WORLD

HUMAN RIGHTS

IN THE MODERN WORLD

by

ARTHUR N. HOLCOMBE

EATON PROFESSOR OF THE SCIENCE OF GOVERNMENT
HARVARD UNIVERSITY

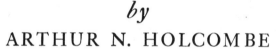

NEW YORK
NEW YORK UNIVERSITY PRESS, WASHINGTON SQUARE
LONDON
GEOFFREY CUMBERLEGE, OXFORD UNIVERSITY PRESS
1948

PRINTED IN THE UNITED STATES OF AMERICA

Contents

Foreword

THE James Stokes Lectureship on Politics has presented to the world a number of impressive studies. No single past publication, I venture to suggest, has dealt more opportunely with an outstanding current issue than the series of lectures by Professor Arthur Norman Holcombe, delivered in March and April of 1948, upon the subject of *Human Rights in the Modern World*.

It is true—as, indeed, Mrs. Eleanor Roosevelt has told the public—that the Russians in their discussion of human rights stress social and economic rights, such as housing, medical care, and social security, while Americans and, I take it, their English ancestors have struggled for individual rights.

But it is likewise true that Englishmen and Americans have under varying circumstances shown tendencies to change emphasis: liberty to an eighteenth-century English statesman may well have seemed to be dependent upon the individual's right to participate in politics. Charles James Fox, friend of the American colonists, declared among other things for universal manhood suffrage. Will Cobbett, emphasizing the same principle in the early nineteenth century, proclaimed his countryman to be a veritable slave, did he not possess the right to vote. And William E. Gladstone, contending for an extension of the franchise in the middle of the sixties, warned his Parliamentary colleagues that additional voters were not to be regarded as representatives of mischief and danger; they were not to be looked upon as armed men within some Trojan horse, bent upon ruin, plunder, and conflagration. Here was no *monstrum infelix* of which it could be said

> ". . . . scandit fatalis machina muros,
>   Foeta armis: mediaeque minans illabitur urbi."

Rather those to whom voting rights might be extended were to be welcomed as men welcome recruits to their armies or children to their families. Two decades later, however, groups of Her Majesty's subjects were displaying interest in a socialistic philosophy. The historian probably will not find it difficult to explain the shift. But, if in more recent days British leaders have come to accept a compromise of these rather divergent outlooks, then can it be assumed that a Western world and an Eastern world will discover the necessity for basing the theory and practice of human rights upon a broad foundation.

Professor Holcombe will tell his story in his own proper way, hoping thereby to contribute to the building of a better organized international community, one more capable of rendering the services needed by mankind in this strenuous age in which we still live. His conclusions will be the conclusions of a scholar whose efforts to promote greater respect for human rights throughout the world and to argue for what seems to him to be the most promising method of proceeding to promote such respect have met with wide recognition.

JOSEPH H. PARK

New York University

The Proposed International Bill of Rights

MAY I not begin with a quotation? It expresses with striking simplicity a general proposition, which most people believe to be true, and a specific observation, which is more debatable. This observation is one that I personally believe to be no less true than the general proposition which it follows. The quotation is of interest also because of the character of its source. It comes from a recent annual report of the Standard Oil Company of New Jersey [1] and reads as follows: "If we are to have a world at peace, we must make substantial and steady progress toward elimination of the underlying causes of war—chief among them poverty and want, prejudice, fear, and the suppression of the rights of man." It is to this last observation—the suppression of the rights of man regarded as an underlying cause of war— that I particularly invite your attention. For a great effort is in the making to give human rights a new and better status in the modern world.

The language of the Charter of the United Nations reflects an impressive show of confidence on the part of the Charter's framers in the wisdom of an attempt to frame an international bill of rights. Seven times altogether, once in the Preamble and six times in the body of the Charter, its framers expressed their faith in fundamental human rights and their determination to secure the blessings of their possession to the peoples of the world. First, in the Preamble, speaking in the name of the peoples of the United Nations, the framers expressed the determination "to re-

The Notes to this lecture begin on page 152.

I

affirm faith in fundamental human rights, in the dignity and worth of the human person," and "in the equal rights of men and women and of nations large and small." The body of the Charter gives repeated evidence of the strength of this determination. Article 1, dealing expressly with the purposes of the United Nations, states that one of them is "to achieve international cooperation . . . . in promoting and encouraging respect for human rights and for fundamental freedoms for all without distinction as to race, sex, language, or religion." Thus was added to the general affirmation of faith in human rights, set forth in the Preamble, an explicit pledge to put an end to discrimination among peoples on account of race, sex, language, or religion.

Article 13 of the Charter, relating to the functions and powers of the General Assembly, imposes a special responsibility upon this organ of the United Nations in fulfillment of its members' purpose concerning human rights. It provides that "the General Assembly shall initiate studies and make recommendations for the purpose of . . . . assisting in the realization of human rights and fundamental freedoms for all without distinction as to race, sex, language, or religion." There is nothing about human rights in the articles that deal with the Security Council, but Article 55, dealing with international economic and social co-operation, contains further evidence of the framers' determination to secure to the peoples of the world a greater measure of freedom. It provides that "with a view to the creation of conditions of stability and well-being which are necessary for peaceful and friendly relations among nations based on respect for the principle of equal rights and self-determination of peoples, the United Nations shall promote . . . . universal respect for, and observance of, human rights and fundamental freedoms for all without distinction as to race, sex, language, or religion." This article adds the obligation to promote the observance of human rights as well as universal respect for them. It plainly implies that the United Nations is to concern itself with matters which might otherwise be regarded as essentially within the jurisdiction of its members, matters in which the United Nations are not authorized under the Charter to intervene. Article 56, by which all members of the United Nations pledge themselves to co-operate for the achievement of the purposes set forth in Article 55, lends further support to the inference that something more is expected of the United Nations than a mere affirmation of respect for the rights of man.

The implications of the Charter are further spelled out in Article 62, dealing with the functions and powers of the Economic and Social Council. By this article the Economic and Social Council is authorized to "make recommendations for the purpose of promoting respect for, and observance of, human rights and fundamental freedoms for all." By Article 68 it is specifically provided that the Economic and Social Council shall set up a commission for the promotion of human rights. Finally, by Article 76, relating to the international trusteeship system, it is declared that one of "the basic objectives of the trusteeship system, in accordance with the Purposes of the United Nations laid down in Article 1 of the present Charter, shall be . . . . to encourage respect for human rights and for fundamental freedoms for all without distinction as to race, sex, language, or religion." For such territories as may be placed under the trusteeship system the obligation of the United Nations to promote respect for, and observance of, human rights is at least as great as that imposed by the Charter upon members of the United Nations in their relations with their own peoples.

The promotion of respect for human rights was manifestly one of the primary concerns of the framers of the Charter. It is one of the few specific activities of the United Nations for which a special administrative agency is expressly authorized. Like the Military Staff Committee, provided to assist the Security Council in making plans for the application of armed force, this agency is charged with the performance of a function that was obviously deemed of high importance in the achievement of the purposes of the framers. How much more may be implied by certain general provisions of the Charter is a matter that can only be determined by future experience. Much or little may be made of the provisions of Article 14, which authorizes the General Assembly to "recommend measures for the peaceful adjustment of any situation, regardless of origin, which it deems likely to impair the general welfare or friendly relations among nations, including situations resulting from a violation of the provisions of the present Charter setting forth the Purposes and Principles of the United Nations." It is not difficult to imagine that under this article discrimination by any nation against some of its own subjects on account of their race or religion might be deemed by the General Assembly likely to impair friendly relations with other nations and hence become the basis for the recommendation of measures of some kind involving action by the United Nations to put a stop to such discrimination. Whatever may be the case with regard to racial or religious discrimination by self-governing nations against minorities within their own borders, it is clear that the United Nations has assumed special obligations with regard to such discrimination in nonself-governing territories.

These provisions of the United Nations Charter were not the result of any sudden impulse on the part of delegates to the United Nations Conference on International Organization. They were the culmination of a long period of preliminary planning by statesmen whose belief in human rights was a part of the foundations of their international policies. The original source of these policies was President Roosevelt's annual message to Congress on January 6, 1941. It was on this occasion that he first made a public statement of the celebrated Four Freedoms, freedom of speech and expression, freedom of worship, freedom from want, and freedom from fear. The last two of these freedoms were explicitly reaffirmed the following August in the Atlantic Charter and received a wide sanction on January 1, 1942,

4

in the Joint Declaration of the United Nations. This declaration made the preservation of human rights one of the principal war aims of the United Nations. President Roosevelt in his annual message to Congress on January 6, 1942, again made clear his conviction that the establishment and security of the Four Freedoms was one of the American objectives in the war.

President Roosevelt's first statement of the Four Freedoms will bear frequent repetition. "We look forward," he wrote, "to a world founded upon four essential human freedoms. The first is freedom of speech and expression—everywhere in the world. The second is freedom of every person to worship God in his own way—everywhere in the world. The third is freedom from want—which, translated into world terms, means economic understandings which will secure to every nation a healthy peaceful life for its inhabitants—everywhere in the world. The fourth is freedom from fear—which, translated into world terms, means a world-wide reduction of armaments to such a point and in such a thorough fashion that no nation will be in a position to commit an act of physical aggression against any neighbor—anywhere in the world."

The President recognized that the last two of these four freedoms were of a different nature from the first two. The first two involve limitations upon the authority of governments for the protection of individuals; the last two involve affirmative action by governments in the service of their peoples. The former are negative, the latter, positive commitments. The President recognized also that something more would be required in order that the full significance of these positive commitments should be understood by the American people. Doubtless with his encouragement, if not at his instigation, the National Resources Planning Board in a report in December of the same year produced an elaboration of the idea of freedom from want. It was in the form of what the Board called a New Bill of Rights, consisting of nine sections. The character of this New Bill of

Rights is suggested by its first and last items. The first was the right to work, usefully and creatively through the productive years, and the last was the right to rest, recreation, and adventure, the opportunity to enjoy life, and to take part in an advancing civilization. Plainly such rights as these are radically different from the time-honored civil rights set forth in the state papers of the American Revolution, although something of the sort may perhaps be implied in the inalienable right to the pursuit of happiness proclaimed in the Declaration of Independence.

The report of the National Resources Planning Board, which Congress permitted to die a few months later for lack of funds, did not attract much attention in the excitement of a war which at the time was far from won. The President, however, continued to be mindful of his obligation to explain more clearly what he meant by his Four Freedoms, particularly the last two of them. In an address to Congress on January 11, 1944, he gave utterance to his further thinking on the nature of freedom from want. "We have come to a clear realization of the fact," he declared, "that true individual freedom cannot exist without economic security and independence. 'Necessitous men are not freemen.' People who are hungry and out of a job are the stuff of which dictatorships are made."

"In our day," the President continued, "these economic truths have become accepted as self-evident. We have accepted, so to speak, a second Bill of Rights under which a new basis of security and prosperity can be established for all—regardless of station, race, or creed.

"Among these are:

"The right to a useful and remunerative job in the industries or shops or farms or mines of the Nation;

"The right of every farmer to raise and sell his products at a return which will give him and his family a decent living;

"The right of every businessman, large and small, to trade in an atmosphere of freedom from unfair competition and domination by monopolies at home or abroad;

6

"The right of every family to a decent home;

"The right to adequate medical care and the opportunity to achieve and enjoy good health;

"The right to adequate protection from the economic fears of old age, sickness, accident, and unemployment;

"The right to a good education."

The President concluded by asking Congress to explore the means for implementing this economic bill of rights.[2] This statement was an impressive improvement, from the standpoint of popular comprehension, upon the New Bill of Rights formulated by the National Resources Planning Board, but it still remained a statement of a goal to be achieved or, rather, a program of legislation better suited for the guidance of a political party than for the immediate inspiration of a people at war. It could not touch the mystic chords of memory like the first two of the Four Freedoms.

President Roosevelt never expounded his conception of the freedom from fear in similarly specific terms. His actions, however, spoke louder than any words. His sponsorship of the Dumbarton Oaks Conference and his planning at the Yalta Conference made clear his purpose to achieve freedom from fear by the establishment of a general international organization for the ends that were eventually set forth in the Preamble of the United Nations Charter. The leadership of President Roosevelt and of those who joined with him in founding the United Nations stimulated worldwide interest in framing an international bill of rights which would voice the aspirations of the modern world as dramatically as had been done in 1789 by the French Declaration of the Rights of Man and of the Citizen. This new international bill of rights should give the Four Freedoms the sanction of the organized opinion of mankind.

Congress has not yet attempted to prepare an economic bill of rights. Perhaps its leaders felt that their duty was done by ratifying the Charter of the United Nations and passing the United Nations Participation Act. The long debate over the Employment Act of 1946 discloses differences of opinion within Congress which would have caused grave difficulties if congressmen had tried to agree upon an interpretation of the freedom from want. Certainly a Congress that was unwilling to vote for a measure called a full-employment bill or to leave in its text any reference to a right to work would not have sanctioned a new bill of rights by which it might have been committed to a far-reaching and highly controversial program of economic and social legislation. Congressmen seemed well content to shift the responsibility for further action, designed to give substance to the new freedom from want, to the same international organization that was charged with the task of implementing the new freedom from fear.

The United Nations, in undertaking to frame an international bill of rights, assumes a task fraught with greater difficulties than those which the American Congress refused to face. There are three reasons for this view. First, the interests of the various members of the United Nations are more diverse than those within the United States. The world is wide, and filled with peoples of many different kinds. It is not only the Americans and the Russians who do not see eye to eye. Consider, for instance, the Republic of Iceland and the Imamate of Yemen. They are also members of the United Nations. Icelanders and Yemenites need not quarrel over the size of their respective armaments, since neither is a menace to the other, but the exploitation of the herring fisheries and the cultivation of the date palm are two very different enterprises. Both herring fishermen and date-growers are likely to be interested in open markets and high prices for their own particular products, but life on a half-frozen island in the upper North Atlantic is very different from life in the torrid deserts of southern Arabia, and each people has long been preoccupied with its own local problems. There are many peoples among the fifty-eight United Nations whose ways of life are almost as diverse as those of Iceland and Yemen, and the variety of interests among them does not facilitate agreement upon basic human rights, if we consider such rights to be identical with vital interests secured by law.

The variety of opinion among the peoples of the United Nations is even more striking than the variety of interests. Herein lies the second reason for believing that the United Nations has assumed a difficult task. The rival merits of capitalism and communism fill a big place in contemporary international controversy, but neither Icelanders nor Yemenites need be greatly concerned with the merits of this particular controversy. The traditional differences between Islam and Christendom reach deeper than those between capitalists and communists. Catholic or Protestant Christians and Shiite or Sunnite Moslems have more to learn about one another in order to reach a common basis of understanding in their international relations than communists and capitalists. The meaning of freedom of speech or of worship to each of these peoples must be found in their respective histories and cultures. The power of a new ideal, such as freedom from want or from fear, in either country will reflect the peculiar experience of its people. If the differences between communism and capitalism loom large in the international politics of Icelanders and Yemenites as well as of all the other lesser peoples of the United Nations, the explanation is not far to seek. It obviously lies less in the nature of their respective national interests than in the consequences of the different interests and opinions among the five major powers.

The different attitudes of the five major powers toward bills of rights in their own systems of government supply the third reason for believing that the United Nations has assumed a task of great difficulty in undertaking to promote universal agreement on an international bill of rights. To frame an international bill of rights, which may become the basis for effective action by the Security Council of the United Nations, involves in the first instance an agreement among the five major powers. No two of these attaches the same importance to a bill of rights at home. Indeed none

of the other major powers attempts to give to the fundamental freedoms of its citizens the same kind of protection
that we attempt to give in the United States. They do not
even appear to agree on which freedoms are fundamental.

The English Bill of Rights is a century older than the
American and even less well adapted to the needs of the
present age. The original American Bill of Rights has been
radically modified by subsequent amendments to the Constitution, although no attempt has yet been made by Congress
to adapt it to the needs of the postwar world, but the
English have made no attempt, at least since the Act of
Settlement in 1701, to make formal changes in the content
of their original Bill. Great changes have been made by
subsequent legislation in the substance of the rights of
Englishmen. Fox's Libel Act, which followed the original
Bill by more than a hundred years, gave much better security
for one of the most important of the fundamental freedoms,
and there has been additional important legislation through
the succeeding century and a half. But in England, as in the
United States, there has been no attempt to express in
formal amendments to the original Bill of Rights the growing popular interest and faith in new freedoms, such as
President Roosevelt suggested for his economic bill of
rights. There is not even agreement between the two great
English-speaking countries on the essentials of due process
of law. Indeed, the English appear much less interested than
we Americans in any formal distinction between fundamental freedoms and the ordinary rights of British subjects
which may be changed at any time by the party in power.

In France the first draft of the new constitution of the
Fourth Republic contained an elaborate declaration of
rights. It was based upon the original Declaration of 1789,
to which was added what President Roosevelt would have
called an economic bill of rights. This draft was the product
of a series of compromises between the three major parties
which dominated French politics in the first year after the
Liberation. The result of the compromises was on the whole

more satisfactory, or less unsatisfactory, to the Socialists and Communists than to the more conservative Popular Republicans. The Socialists had striven to hold the balance between the left and right parties so as to make the new constitution acceptable to both. The Communists, true to their Soviet prototype, seemed to care less about fundamental human rights than either of the other parties, but objected strongly to certain important concessions to the Rightists, particularly in such matters as the status of private property and of religious schools. The Rightists found the concessions inadequate and their opposition caused the defeat of the proposed constitution at the polls.

In preparing the second draft of the new constitution, the Socialists, who continued to hold the balance between the left and the right and could not evade their responsibility for the final decisions, sought to end the controversies which had wrecked their first effort by omitting the declaration of rights. This was what had been done also under similar circumstances by the framers of the constitutional laws of the Third Republic. Instead of a formal declaration of rights, they framed a preamble, solemnly guaranteeing the rights and freedoms consecrated by the Declaration of Rights of 1789 and also the fundamental principles recognized by the laws of the republic, whatever those might be, to which they added an informal list of economic and social principles, proclaimed as most vital in our time. This expedient saved the substance of a modified economic bill of rights, and enabled the constitution to gain the grudging approval of a majority of Frenchmen at the polls. The result was a precarious compromise between the ideas of the Rightists and the Leftists. It was not satisfactory even to the Socialists in the political center but it saved the constitution from a second defeat at the polls. The preamble, however, could not possess the practical importance in the law of the land of a formal declaration embodied in the text of the constitution. As often before in history, the platform of a political party did duty as a formulation of basic principles of right.

The Communist rulers of the Soviet Union have shown less interest in what the French in their new constitution call the "inalienable and sacred rights" of "every human being." The Soviet Union constitution of 1923, or so-called Lenin constitution, contained no declaration or bill of rights. In the Stalin constitution of 1936 there is a chapter setting forth the fundamental rights and duties of Soviet citizens, but, unlike the declarations and bills of rights in constitutions framed in the Western political tradition, this Russian bill of rights is not emphasized by receiving the first place in the constitution. Chapter I of the Stalin constitution deals with the organization of society, which its framers manifestly regarded as of the highest importance in the fundamental law, and the statement concerning the fundamental rights and duties of citizens does not appear until Chapter X. The Russian Communists, consistent with their version of Marxist political science, regard a declaration of rights as less important than a right constitution of the foundations of society on which, as they believe, the rights of man depend for any real existence.

The Communist point of view is illustrated by the document which, in Soviet constitutional history, may best be compared with the French Declaration of 1789. This is the Declaration of Rights of the Toiling and Exploited Peoples, adopted by the All-Russian Congress of Soviets in January 1918. This declaration states that the fundamental aim of the Revolution is "to suppress all exploitation of man by man, to abolish forever the division of society into classes . . . . and to bring about the socialist organization of society in all countries." This aim was to be pursued in the first instance by abolishing private property in land and in the means of production, by establishing workers' control of industry, and by nationalizing the banks. The framers of this declaration of rights proceeded to express confidence in the Soviets as organs of representative government, and concluded that "at the decisive moment in the struggle of the proletariat with its exploiters the latter can have no place in any of the organs of power." The framers of such a declaration could doubtless have joined in a statement of a purpose to achieve international co-operation in promoting respect for human rights without distinction as to race, sex, language, or religion, but they could not have joined in a renunciation of distinctions on account of social position or ownership of property. To them the equal protection of the laws would mean something very different from its meaning in the United States.

The last of the powers with a veto in the Security Council is China. In modern times the Chinese have borrowed freely from the West, from Washington and New York as well as from London and Paris, Berlin and Moscow, but behind these ideas recently borrowed from the West lies a long heritage of native ideas and indigenous political institutions, which inevitably predispose the Chinese to a characteristic attitude of their own toward the problem of drafting an international bill of rights. In a part of the world where individual rights have traditionally been subordinated to those of the family, the adjustment of the relations between the individual and the state has been less important than the adjustments between the family and the state. In such a land the whole problem of defining basic human rights and fundamental freedoms takes a peculiar form. The willingness of the Chinese to introduce Western concepts of liberty and law should simplify the problem of formulating basic human rights and fundamental freedoms in a manner acceptable to the Chinese, but it ought not to be expected that rights intended to be reduced to practice should be regarded in precisely the same light by the peoples of the Far East and of the West. In fact, the bill of rights provided for the new Chinese constitution of 1947 is a compromise between the political ideas of different parts of the West. American ideas seem to be dominant. But the most important characteristic is the domination of the spirit of compromise itself. There is no important right in the chapter of this new constitution on the rights of citizens that is not dependent for its practical effect upon the enactment of an enforcement bill by the Legislative Yuan.

It is evident that an international bill of rights, which is designed to furnish a basis for action by the Security Council, will have to be a compromise between compromises. Even the Russian bill of rights, if Chapter X of the Stalin constitution may be so described, seems to be a compromise between the ideas of those who believed all bills of rights to be incompatible with the dictatorship of the Communists and those who would have gone further in saluting the faith of Western democrats in basic human rights. An international bill of rights, which both Russians and Americans are to ratify and join in carrying into effect, apparently cannot be both comprehensive and explicit. It may be comprehensive, but if both capitalists and communists are to subscribe to it will it not have to be ambiguous? Or it may be clear and luminous, but will it not have to be limited to those matters of universal concern in which capitalists and communists feel a common interest? It would seem that the members of the United Nations must choose, if they expect their fundamental freedoms to be safeguarded by the agencies they have established under the Charter.

If it is not action by the General Assembly and Security Council that is the principal objective in framing an international bill of rights, but rather a declaration of rights that may serve as a guide to action by the individual members of the United Nations, then it will not be necessary to make so many compromises on matters of principle for the sake of conciliating opposition by the various major powers. But it will still be necessary to frame a declaration that can command the approval of at least two thirds of the members in the General Assembly. It will have to be acceptable to the Latin-American states, since they possess more than a third of the votes in the General Assembly. It ought not to be deemed too unsuitable by the Moslem states, since there are ten of them, enough to constitute an important bloc in the deliberations of the General Assembly. But the Latin-American states cannot approve a declaration that is belligerent toward dictators, since dictatorship is a normal form of government among them, and the Moslem states have inherited a theory of law that has never been hospitable to the Western practice of experimental legislation. The common ground upon which all the peoples of the United Nations may take their stand together is not broad enough to support all the freedoms that may be deemed fundamental by Americans, Englishmen, Frenchmen, Russians, Chinese, Hindus, Moslems, and others with their various traditions and peculiar views concerning the nature of basic human rights.

It must be conceded that, as Professor Lauterpacht [3] puts it with scholarly restraint, "Any attempt to translate the idea of an international bill of rights of man into a working rule of law is fraught with difficulties which disturb orthodox thought to the point of discouragement." These difficulties are of three kinds. The first is the difficulty of agreement upon the content of such a bill. The second is the difficulty of enforcement. The third is what Professor Lauterpacht calls the political difficulty. Evidently what is involved in any declaration of rights is a definition of the relation of the individual to the society in which he lives. How far is an international bill of rights compatible with the principle that the people of each state must be left free to manage their own domestic affairs? In view of all these difficulties, to continue to borrow the sober language of Professor Lauterpacht,[4] "It may be felt that indulgence in the idea of an international bill of the rights of man is a regrettable dispersion of effort, of the futility and utter impracticability of which the student of law and politics ought to warn both governments and public opinion at large."

Despite the warnings of Professor Lauterpacht and others, scholars and jurists in many countries have tried their hand at drafting an international bill of rights. Among the many such productions abroad none is more interesting to Americans than that produced by Professor Lauterpacht himself and explained in his valuable book, *An International Bill of the Rights of Man.* In our own country the outstanding efforts have been the work of groups of scholars united for the purpose of producing more deliberate drafts than could be produced by any single writer. Among these, the most noteworthy are the Statement of Essential Human Rights, prepared by a committee of the American Law Institute and published in January 1946,[5] and the Draft International Bill of Human Rights, prepared by the Committee on Human Rights of the American Association for the United Nations and published by the Carnegie Endowment for International Peace in December of the same year.[6] The former was described by its authors as a "declaration" designed "to express those freedoms to which every human being is entitled and to assure that all shall live under a government of the people, by the people, for the people." The latter was not designed to be a mere declaration but a genuine bill, which could be incorporated into the law of nations and also into the laws of particular nations.

The two plans are remarkably alike in substance. The former contains eighteen separate articles; the latter, nineteen. Sixteen of the eighteen articles in the statement of the American Law Institute's committee cover substantially the same ground as seventeen of the nineteen articles in the draft of the committee of the American Association for the United Nations. They cover the time-honored freedoms of religion, of opinion, of speech, and of assembly, the right to form associations, immunity against unreasonable searches and seizures and other wrongful interferences with the person, home, reputation, or property of the individual, the right to a fair trial, and to freedom from arbitrary detention, immunity against retroactive laws, and the equal protection of the laws. In addition, both contained several articles appropriate for a new economic bill of rights. Among these were articles setting forth a right to education, a right to work, and a right to social security. The statement by the American Law Institute's committee contained also a right to own property under general law, which was not included in the draft bill of the other committee, and a right to adequate food and housing, which the other committee likewise omitted. Strong objections to the recognition of the first of these two rights would obviously be made by the government of one of the greatest powers in the modern world, and perhaps also by others among the major powers. A right to adequate food and housing would presumably not be challenged by any important government in the modern world, but it may have seemed to the other drafting committee so incontestable as the statement of a humanitarian goal and so uncertain as a guide for action in the choice of public policies as to be out of place in a list of essential human rights.

The Draft International Bill of Human Rights prepared under the direction of the American Association for the United Nations recognizes that the practical significance of fundamental freedoms of any kind will depend upon the provisions for their actual observance. The draft international bill, therefore, provided that these rights should be deemed fundamental principles of international law and of the national law of each of the members of the United Nations, principles that would be realized by appropriate action by international and national agencies. This draft international bill concluded with an exhortation to the members of the United Nations to provide effective measures for the enforcement of these essential human rights, and to the United Nations as an organized body to take measures for executing the provisions of the Charter designed to safeguard these rights throughout the world. What these measures should be, however, is not indicated in the draft. The choice of measures was tacitly left for determination by the United Nations in pursuance of its duties under the Charter.

Professor Lauterpacht's draft of an international bill of rights went further than either of the American drafts in the effort to deal effectively with the problem of enforcement. It distinguished between the provisions that he deemed enforceable in the law courts of member states of the United Nations and those that seemed to him not enforceable in that manner. These two kinds of provisions he placed in two separate parts of his draft. Finally, in a third part of the draft he dealt more explicitly with the problem of enforcement. Every state, he stipulated, should incorporate Part I of the bill into its own body of fundamental laws, but Part II of the bill was to stand as an ideal for the purpose of inspiring the peoples of the world to demand its realization as fast as circumstances might make that practicable. Neither Professor Lauterpacht nor the authors of the American drafts attempted to solve the third of the three problems raised by the provisions of the United Nations Charter relating to human rights; namely, that of the compatibility of international efforts to promote universal respect for human rights with the right of every sovereign people to determine for themselves what shall be the relation between the individual and the society in which he lives. This problem was tacitly left for further consideration at a more convenient time.

The members of the United Nations Conference on International Organization at San Francisco understood the difficulties of their task. They wisely rejected all proposals for including an international declaration or bill of rights in the Charter itself. But they did not ignore the problems involved in any serious effort to promote universal respect for basic human rights. They were clearly aware of the need for a sound approach to the solution of these problems. The evidence of this awareness is the article in the Charter specifically requiring the Economic and Social Council to set up a commission on human rights.

As soon as the United Nations Organization had been formed, its officers lost no time in beginning to fulfill the obligations under the Charter to promote universal respect for, and observance of, human rights. At the first session of the General Assembly the Economic and Social Council was established. This organ of the United Nations seized the first opportunity to discharge the duty imposed upon the United Nations by Article 68 of the Charter. The first step was the appointment of a temporary committee, the so-called Nuclear Commission, to plan a program of work in the field of human rights. Later in the year the Nuclear Commission reported that a permanent commission on human rights should be established and that among other tasks it should prepare an international bill of rights to be promulgated under the authority of the United Nations. This report was accepted by the Economic and Social Council, and in October 1946 the establishment of a permanent United Nations Commission on Human Rights was duly authorized. The members of the Commission were appointed before the end of the year, and its first session took place in January 1947.

The Commission on Human Rights promptly appointed a Drafting Committee to examine materials prepared for its consideration by the Secretariat and also the materials received from private sources. The Drafting Committee held a formal session in June of 1947 and adopted a tentative program for submission to the Commission on Human Rights at its second regular meeting in December at Geneva. At this session, which extended from December 2 to December 17, there was an extended debate in which the implications of its assignment were thoroughly explored from all points of view. The Commission then divided its task into three parts. The first dealt with the determination of the contents of an international bill of rights; the second, with the problem of enforcement; and the third, with the political problem, that is, the problem involved in an effort to give practical effect to universal standards of right in the various countries of the world with their various and by no means consistent systems of government and law.

It was decided to apply the term, an International Bill of Rights, to the entirety of the document in preparation. This comprised, first, a declaration of rights to be adopted by the General Assembly of the United Nations; secondly, a covenant to be included in a convention, to be ratified by the members of the United Nations and embodied in their several codes of law; and, thirdly, a report on measures for implementation in which the relations between the United Nations and its various members, growing out of efforts to enforce respect for and observance of human rights, might be determined. In pursuance of its program the Commission on Human Rights at its session in December 1947 tentatively adopted a proposed Declaration of Rights, containing thirty-three articles and covering most, but not all, of the topics that members of the commission deemed suitable for inclusion in such a declaration. It also adopted tentatively a Covenant on Human Rights, containing twenty-seven articles deemed appropriate by a majority of its members for inclusion in an international convention. The Commission failed to bring its study of implementation to a conclusion.

There were wide differences of opinion within the Commission. The American view, represented by Mrs. Franklin D. Roosevelt, disclosed a feeling that the proposed drafts were too ambitious, attempting to reach a more comprehensive and explicit formulation of human rights than is practicable under the complex circumstances of the modern world. The Russian delegates, on the other hand, were of the opinion that the proposed draft of an international declaration of human rights did not go far enough and that it was impossible to reach agreement on the contents of an international covenant until agreement had been reached on the contents of an international declaration. The Russian spokesman also thought that it was useless to discuss measures for the implementation of an international bill of rights until agreement should be reached on the contents of the proposed Declaration and the proposed Covenant. It is evident that the framing of an international bill of rights is still in an early stage and that wide differences of opinion remain to be ironed out before agreement can be reached and constructive action taken to promote universal respect for and observance of human rights. The Draft International Declaration on Human Rights and the Draft International Covenant on Human Rights, however, were published for consideration by the peoples of the world, and the Commission on Human Rights adjourned to meet again in May for the consideration of the comments by the governments of the member nations and others on these tentative proposals.

This report of the United Nations Commission on Human Rights reveals its members' awareness of the difficulties inherent in its task. The difficulty of choosing between an international declaration of rights, as recommended by the committee of the American Law Institute, and an international bill of rights in the strict sense of the term, as recommended by the committee of the American Association for the United Nations, was avoided by the simple expedient of declining to make such a choice. The Commission on Human Rights followed the Lauterpacht plan and adopted drafts of both a declaration and a bill or, to adopt the Commission's terminology, a covenant. The former, if approved by the Economic and Social Council and by the General Assembly, may be proclaimed under the sponsorship of the United Nations as the expression of the organized opinion of mankind. The latter, embodied in a convention suitable for ratification by the member nations, may become a part of the law of nations, or at least a part of the laws of the ratifying states. The former, if well suited to its purpose, might become one of the great state papers which have played so influential a part in the political education of many peoples. The latter would depend for its practical efficacy upon the solution of the problem of enforcement.

Before attempting to estimate the chances of success in the effort by the United Nations to perform its duty under the Charter, to promote respect for, and observance of, human rights and fundamental freedoms in the contentious world in which we live, we should turn our attention to the development of the idea of fundamental human rights in our own country, and examine the progress that has been made in the practical realization of such rights under the Constitution of the United States. We wish to know what light is thrown by the experience of the United States upon the solution of the three great practical problems raised by the program of the United Nations for promoting respect for basic human rights: first, the problem of a suitable content for an international bill of rights; secondly, the problem of enforcement; and, thirdly, the problem of reconciling the obligations of membership in a particular political community with the requirements of a universal system of human rights. Then, in the light of American experience, the attempt can be made to appraise the character and estimate the prospects of the International Bill of Rights submitted by the United Nations Commission on Human Rights to the inspection and criticism of mankind.

The American Bill of Rights

THE idea of an international bill of rights is a direct descendant of ideas cherished by the American and French revolutionists of the eighteenth century.[1] They, too, believed in the rights of man and in the practical capacity of men living in an age of reason to realize such rights. These ideas in turn descended from ideas cherished by the English revolutionists of the seventeenth century. The English Revolution of 1688, which Englishmen still like to call the Glorious Revolution, gave two important state papers to the history of human rights. One was the Declaration of Right; the other, the Bill of Rights.[2]

The distinction suggested by the change of title is as significant in modern times as it was in the time of William and Mary and the Convention Parliament. The Declaration of Right contained the articles of agreement between the new sovereign and the Parliament concerning the conditions upon which the latter would put the former on the throne. The Bill of Rights possessed substantially the same content. Both set forth certain rights and liberties which the previous king had been unwilling to respect and which Parliament deemed essential to the peace and safety of the realm. But the principles embodied in the Declaration of Right rested solely upon the good faith of the parties to the agreement. There was no sanction for their enforcement other than the interest of the new rulers in observing the conditions upon which they had received their crowns and that of the Whig and Tory partisans in maintaining a policy that they could not safely abandon while the general political situation remained unchanged. Whether an appeal to public opinion

The Notes to this lecture begin on page 152.

could give additional security for keeping the agreement was highly debatable in a period when there was no general freedom of the press and no real freedom of speech except for Members of Parliament.

The authors of the Bill of Rights sought greater security for the rights and liberties contained in the Declaration of Right by putting it in the form of an act of Parliament and thus embodying them in the law of the land. The effect of this action was to enable the judges to take notice of these rights, whenever cases involving infractions of them should be brought into the courts of law. Thus the Bill of Rights added a judicial sanction to that previously and precariously provided by public opinion, or rather by the opinion of the Whig party in English politics. To make this judicial sanction more effective the Whig leaders took advantage of the opportunity, furnished by the subsequent necessity of an Act of Settlement to determine finally the title to the throne, to give the judges better protection against removal from office by the Crown. Greater security of tenure, it was expected, would enable judges to become more competent guardians of the liberties of the subject and more useful allies of Parliament in future struggles against tyrants on the throne. In fact, the increased dependence of the judges upon Parliament did make them more independent of the Crown. It was to the Bill of Rights, therefore, rather than to the Declaration of Right that subsequent generations of Englishmen, at least until the time when a genuine freedom of speech and of the press could be established for all Englishmen, chiefly looked for the security of such basic human rights and fundamental freedoms as were asserted by the seventeenth-century English revolutionists.

The English Convention Parliament, its action plainly showed, was more concerned to assert its own rights and to establish its supremacy over the Crown than to increase the rights of ordinary Englishmen. The right of free speech, for instance, was claimed for Members of Parliament engaged in the performance of their constitutional duties, but not for members of the general public outside of Parliament. In fact, the general public was not allowed to know what was going on within the houses of Parliament at Westminster. The secrecy of debates was undoubtedly a protection for Parliament men threatened with persecution for their political opinions by imperious sovereigns, but it was of only indirect and speculative value to ordinary Englishmen who might at times lack confidence in partisans entrenched behind the walls of the houses of Parliament as well as in princes upon their thrones. Some rights were extended to others besides Parliamentarians, but not to all the people. The right to bear arms, for instance, was reserved to that part of the people who were Protestants, but denied to Catholics. There was recognition of the possibility of oppression by a king, but no recognition of such a possibility by a parliament, or by a political party possessing a majority of the votes in a parliament.

The English Bill of Rights laid a solid foundation for the reign of law in that country instead of the arbitrary rule of men upon a throne. This it accomplished particularly by denying to the Crown the power to suspend the laws, or to tamper with the processes established by law for the administration of justice. Procedural rights gained greater respect than ever before, but substantive limitations upon the authority of Parliament, as distinct from that of the Crown, were not deemed necessary. It is significant that the right of ordinary subjects to petition for the redress of grievances was protected in so far as the petitions might be directed to the King, but nothing was said of a right to petition Parliament. By the Bill of Rights Parliament successfully asserted its freedom to protect the subject against the Crown, but the freedom of the subject to protect himself continued to leave a great deal to be desired.

The American revolutionists, who framed the first declarations and bills of rights in the United States, were aware of the limitations as well as the achievements of the English revolutionists. They understood clearly enough that the

English Whigs were not trying to define the basic human rights of all mankind. The English Whigs, it was plainly evident, essayed a more modest role. They were seeking remedies for specific grievances. They hoped to find them in the form of appropriate limitations on the power of kings.

The American revolutionists faced a different and more difficult problem. They had rid themselves of kings, and were concerned with the need for protection against the abuse of power by themselves, or by representatives of their own choice in the state legislatures. The English had only to proclaim that their former king had broken some of the terms of the social compact. They did not have to explain what other terms might be necessary or proper for such a compact, if it was to supply a satisfactory basis of government for a people who, as Jefferson put it in the Declaration of Independence, were about to assume among the powers of the earth the separate and equal station to which the laws of nature and of nature's God entitled them. The English revolutionists were concerned with only one of the basic human rights, the right of revolution, but the Americans had to reconsider all the fundamental questions that make up the total problem of political obedience. They could readily agree, when agreement became necessary, that they possessed an inalienable right to life, liberty, and the pursuit of happiness, but it was less easy to agree on the plan for pursuing happiness that would have the best prospect of bringing them to the goal. It was doubtless something, in fact as the world stood in 1776 it was a great deal, to declare that the common people had a right to pursue happiness in their own way. But the task remained to discover which way would actually be best and to provide the most favorable conditions for the adoption of the best way.

American experience with the effort to secure basic human rights and fundamental freedoms throughout the Union throws much light on the problem of enforcing in a uniform manner such rights throughout the world. American experience begins with the effort to enforce the rights asserted in the Declaration of Independence. Despite the confident assertion at the beginning of the Declaration that all men are created equal, the facts of life in the United States disclosed the sharpest conflicts with such a principle.[3] As the controversy over the institution of Negro slavery proceeded toward its climax, discussion of the meaning of the Declaration grew heated. Some defenders of slavery attempted to dismiss the problem by referring to these provisions of the Declaration as glittering generalities. Others, more contemptuous of American traditions, dismissed the self-evident truths as self-evident lies. It was one of the achievements of Abraham Lincoln to give in one of his great speeches an answer to this problem that would satisfy the best impulses of the American people.[4]

Lincoln stated his idea of equality as follows: "I think that the authors of that notable instrument [the Declaration of Independence] intended to include all men, but that they did not intend to declare all men equal in all respects. They did not mean to say that all were equal in color, size, intellect, moral development, or social capacity. They defined with tolerable distinctness in what respects they did consider all men created equal—equal in certain inalienable rights, among which are life, liberty, and the pursuit of happiness. This they said and this they meant. They did not mean to assert the obvious untruth, that all men were then actually enjoying that equality, nor yet that they were about to confer it upon them. In fact, they had no power to confer such a boon. They meant simply to declare the right, so that the enforcement of it might follow as fast as circumstances should permit. They meant to set up a standard maxim for free society which should be familiar to all and revered by all—constantly looked to, constantly labored for, and even though never perfectly attained, constantly approximated; and thereby constantly spreading and deepening its influence and augmenting the happiness and value of life to all people, of all colors, everywhere." Thus Lincoln succeeded

27

in reconciling the inalienable rights of the Declaration with the facts of American life. It was evident that the full realization of these rights would depend upon the progress of the political education of the American people.

Political education in the United States, like most other kinds of education, is primarily the responsibility of the states. The first of the state declarations of rights was that written by George Mason and adopted by the Virginia convention of delegates, June 12, 1776. This is officially described as "a declaration of rights made by the representatives of the good People of Virginia; which rights do pertain to them and their posterity as the basis and foundation of government." There were altogether sixteen of these rights. The latest and most carefully prepared of the original state declarations of rights was that adopted by Massachusetts in 1780. This declaration contained thirty separate articles, including substantially everything mentioned in the Virginia declaration together with numerous other rights not claimed by the Virginians. Though the Massachusetts declaration was longer and more comprehensive, the spirit of the two documents and the general character of their contents were essentially the same.[5]

Each begins with a number of general statements about government. The first article of the Virginia declaration, for example, reads as follows: "that all Men are by nature equally free and independent, and have certain inherent Rights, of which, when they enter into a State of Society they cannot, by any Compact deprive or divest their Posterity; namely, the Enjoyment of Life, and Liberty, with the Means of acquiring and Possessing Property, and pursuing and obtaining Happiness and Safety." There are six such general propositions in the Virginia declaration of rights, stating what seemed to its authors to be self-evident truths about government. They were regarded by the revolutionary leaders in Virginia as the essential principles of a government of the people such as they sought to establish.

There follow in the Virginia declaration a number of

other statements about government, which hardly qualify as general principles but fall more properly under the head of good advice about the conduct of public affairs. The seventh article of the Virginia declaration, for instance, states: "that all power of suspending laws or the execution of laws by any authority without consent of the representatives of the people is injurious to these rights and ought not to be exercised." Another one of these articles states simply: "That excessive Bail ought not to be required, nor excessive Fines imposed; nor cruel and unusual Punishments inflicted." More general in character is the advice in Article 15. "No free government," it declared, "or the blessing of liberty, can be preserved to any people but by a firm adherence to justice, moderation, temperance, frugality, and virtue, and by frequent recurrence to fundamental principles." The influence of the English Declaration of Right is clear. But the good advice is not directed to anybody in particular, and there is nothing in the Virginia declaration to suggest that it was intended for public officers any more than for the people at large.

The Virginia declaration of rights contains no clear limitation of any kind on the substantive powers of the state government and only one explicit limitation of a procedural character. This was Article 8, which provided for trial by jury in criminal cases. It also protected the accused against compulsion to give evidence against himself. It concluded with the provision that no man should be deprived of his liberty except by the law of the land or the judgment of his peers. Concerning the proper procedure in civil cases the declaration states merely that "the ancient trial by jury is preferable to any other and ought to be held sacred." In the Massachusetts declaration of rights there is likewise no clear limitation of a substantive character on governmental power and there are only four articles that clearly establish procedural limitations. Like the Virginia declaration that of Massachusetts is largely devoted to the statement of general principles of government and to offering good advice on the conduct of public affairs to the politicians and the people.

In neither of these early state declarations of right is there anything to suggest President Roosevelt's third and fourth freedoms. Freedom from want was not regarded as a general public interest. The poor, whom the general public expected always to have with them, were to be cared for according to their need, but such care was considered to be a public duty rather than a personal right. Freedom from fear was deemed desirable, but it was not fear of foreign foes that was in the minds of the framers of these declarations. Their fear was of domestic tyrants. Their expedient for relieving such a fear was to hold the military power in a proper subordination to the civil authority.

These early state declarations of rights were designed primarily for purposes of political education and for the development of a sound public opinion. Their possible use as the basis for a systematic review of the acts of one set of public officers by another set was evidently not uppermost in the minds of their authors. This is most clearly the case with the article of the Virginia declaration dealing with freedom of conscience. It reads as follows: "That Religion, or the Duty which we owe to our Creator, and the Manner of discharging it, can be directed only by Reason and Conviction, not by Force or Violence; and therefore, all Men are equally entitled to the free Exercise of Religion, according to the Dictates of Conscience; and that it is the mutual Duty of all to practice Christian Forebearance, Love, and Charity, towards each other." There is evidently no general principle of government in this article, but surely an abundance of good advice.

By the inclusion of these declarations of rights in the original state constitutions, however, they became genuine bills of rights, enforceable like other parts of the state constitutions in the courts of law. Since they were parts of the fundamental law, the judges were free to observe their provisions when in conflict with the ordinary law, if they

chose to do so. They did so choose in a number of interesting cases that were decided in the years immediately after
the Revolution. In Massachusetts the judges went so far as
to hold that the general declaration in favor of human
liberty put an end to the institution of Negro slavery without further action by the state legislature. Since the constitution in Massachusetts had been adopted by a special process
which was more difficult than the ordinary process of legislation, the legislature could not easily have maintained its
own interpretation of the constitution against that of the
judges, even if it had wished to do so. Hence, the judges
were in a better position to make their decisions stick than
in England, where Parliament could alter the provisions of
the Bill of Rights by the same process as any other of its
acts.

This was the foundation of the system of judicial review
and judicial veto that put the fundamental freedoms of the
American bills of rights upon a different basis from ordinary statutory privileges and immunities. Judges obviously
would have difficulty in making good their interpretations
of general principles of government, and particularly of the
good advice in which the early state bills of rights abounded,
unless supported by a clear and strong public opinion. In the
latter case, the likelihood of a conflict with the legislature
was small. But in dealing with substantive limitations on
legislative power and with procedural rights, the judges
were in a stronger position. Thus, the limitations on the
power of the legislatures and the procedural rights contained in the state bills of rights tended to gain greater
importance in the normal processes of state government
than those of a more general, though doubtless more basic,
character. The effect was to make possible a considerable
advance over the English Declaration of Right in the treatment of the civil rights of the common people, of which the
most important are included in the first two of President
Roosevelt's Four Freedoms.

If the state bills of rights brought fresh security for the

first two of the Four Freedoms, there was little in them, it should be emphasized, relating to the last two of the Four Freedoms. If freedom from fear be understood as security against the danger of domestic tyranny as well as of foreign aggression, there was provision for it in the Virginia bill of rights. On this point the reference to a right to bear arms was explicit and emphatic. Article 13 provided "that a well regulated militia, composed of the body of the people, trained to arms, is the proper, natural, and safe defence of a free state; that standing armies, in time of peace, should be avoided, as dangerous to liberty; and that, in all cases, the military should be under strict subordination to, and governed by, the civil power." The Massachusetts provision on this point was equally explicit and emphatic. But these were not provisions that could readily be enforced by judges in the courts of law against heedless or misguided legislators. Their principal sanction would have to be public opinion; that is, the good sense and determination of a properly educated people or of their representatives. On this point the influence of the English revolutionists over the American is clear.

Freedom from want was even less well provided for than freedom from fear. There were no provisions in any of the state bills of rights for securing a right to work and nothing about the conditions of employment or what is now called social security. The independent farmers and tradesmen who constituted the bulk of the free population in 1776 were more interested in equality of opportunity to subjugate the wilderness and exploit the natural resources of the country than in what we now call social and industrial justice. Instead of a right to work there was a popular demand for the kind of liberty that consists of leveling natural barriers to profitable enterprise rather than organizing the market for labor and regulating the conditions of employment in the interests of a special class of wage earners. In this area of modern freedom the original state bills of rights registered no advance over that of the English revolutionists.

The American Bill of Rights

There was no declaration of rights in the original draft of the Constitution of the United States. The framers of the Constitution in 1787 were preoccupied with other matters until a week before the end of the Federal Constitutional Convention. On September 12, George Mason, who could not forget his connection with the Virginia bill of rights or the general satisfaction with which it had been received by the public, expressed the wish that there might be a bill of rights also in the federal Constitution.[6] "It would give great quiet," he added, "to the people." Elbridge Gerry of Massachusetts promptly moved that a bill of rights be prepared.

Roger Sherman of Connecticut opposed the motion. According to Madison's report of the debate, Sherman "was for securing the rights of the people where requisite," but he pointed out that the state declarations of rights were not repealed by the federal Constitution, and, he added, "being in force are sufficient." He seemed confident that Congress could be trusted not to violate the rights secured to the people by the state constitutions. Mason rejoined that the laws of the United States would be paramount to state bills of rights. The states represented in the Convention, however, unanimously rejected the motion. Some of the delegates doubtless shared Sherman's confidence in the good intentions of the peoples' representatives. Others, reposing less confidence in the peoples' representatives, evidently possessed little confidence in the practical capacity of a bill of rights to keep them from abusing their power. Others still were weary after a long hot summer of incessant debate and contentiousness. They were impatient for an end of their labors. Mason's suggestion that a bill of rights be included in the Constitution had been prompted by the observation that no provision had been made for trial by jury in civil cases, but the other delegates preferred to omit such a provision rather than to make further effort to agree upon a uniform rule to govern such trials in the federal courts in all parts of the Union. Differences in local customs seemed to make a uniform rule for the federal courts undesirable, if not impracticable.

In the state ratifying conventions the omission of a guarantee of trial by jury in civil cases was promptly noticed and widely condemned. In the Massachusetts convention this omission was discussed at length.[7] The delegates finally decided not to ratify the proposed Constitution without expressing the opinion that amendments were required in order, as the resolution of ratification put it, "to remove the fears and quiet the apprehensions of many of the good people of this Commonwealth." There followed nine specific proposals for additions to or alterations in the proposed Constitution. None of these could be described as a general principle of government or as mere advice to public officers. Each called for an explicit limitation upon the power of Congress or upon the processes for the administration of justice in the federal courts. After this action of the Massachusetts ratifying convention all the state ratifying conventions took similar action.

Some of the state conventions, notably those of Virginia and New York, proposed systematic and comprehensive declarations of popular rights as well as explicit amendments to the body of the federal Constitution.[8] It was evident that fears which needed to be removed and apprehensions that needed to be quieted were widespread among the good people of the states and that the addition of a bill of rights would allay much of the opposition which had developed to the ratification of the Constitution as proposed by the Federal Convention. The plain people, represented more effectively in the state ratifying conventions than in the Federal Convention, were evidently uneasy at the grant of extensive powers to a distant government which would operate largely out of sight and might easily, they seemed to fear, get out of control. There was little agreement concerning specific changes in the proposed frame of government, but a general desire for assurances of some sort that basic human rights and fundamental freedoms would be as secure under the government of the new and more powerful Union as under the familiar governments of the states. In response to this general popular sentiment, therefore, the First Congress under the Constitution proposed the amendments which, when duly ratified, became the federal Bill of Rights.

The content of the federal Bill of Rights, comprising the first ten amendments to the Constitution of the United States, offers a striking contrast to that of the earlier state declarations.[9] Only one of the ten articles, namely, the tenth, sets forth a principle of government and only two others, the eighth and ninth, contain nothing more than may fairly be described as good advice. Article 10 deals with the distribution of power between the federal and state governments. The eighth article repeats the good advice of the Virginia declaration respecting excessive bail and fines and cruel and unusual punishments. The ninth article contains a general statement that "the enumeration in the Constitution of certain rights shall not be construed to deny or disparage others retained by the people." The other articles of the federal Bill of Rights set forth specific limitations upon the powers of the Federal Government. These limitations are both procedural and substantive in character. For example, Article 3 provides both a substantive and a procedural limitation: "No soldier shall, in time of peace, be quartered in any house without the consent of the owner, nor in time of war but in a manner to be prescribed by law." The practice of quartering troops in private houses was abandoned long ago and these particular rights no longer seem important. If it was ever proper to describe the immunity of Americans against unlawful quartering of troops as a basic human right, it certainly would not be so described now.

The other articles of the federal Bill of Rights relate to matters that continue to be of clear and present interest to the American people. Both the substantive and the procedural rights are more numerous, more explicit, and more

35

important than in the state bills of rights. Article 1 of the federal Bill contains a much more comprehensive statement of the freedoms of conscience and of communication than can be found in any of the state bills. It is not put in the mild form of good advice to whomsoever may be persuaded to take notice of its existence and to act according to its spirit. It takes the form of a direct instruction to Congress, commanding that it shall not make any law affecting an establishment of religion or prohibiting the free exercise thereof. It commands further that Congress shall make no law abridging the freedom of speech or of the press, or the right of the people peaceably to assemble and to petition the government for a redress of grievances. Article 2 also contains a substantive limitation on the power of Congress. It declares plainly that the right to keep and bear arms shall not be infringed.

The remaining articles set forth various procedural rights, which, like the preceding limitations on the authority of Congress, relate to matters of which judges can take notice in the course of administering justice. If the judges enjoy due security of tenure, they can give effective protection to such rights, whether the action taken is popular or not. In other words, this portion of the federal Bill of Rights was capable of becoming an instrument for the protection of unpopular minorities against the abuse of power by heedless or misguided majorities, acting through the forms of law but without proper authority under the Constitution. This was a kind of safeguard against oppression which could mean something in a land under a popular government, where the danger of oppression would come from the people themselves, or from their representatives tempted to abuse their power by the hope of gaining greater popularity.

Such a bill of rights resembled rather that of the English Revolution than those adopted by the states during the course of the American Revolution. It dealt mainly with specific grievances, for which it sought practical remedies not dependent for their efficacy upon the uncertain action of public opinion. It sought rather to give the public free access to the facts and arguments upon which a sound public opinion must rest than to give it advice concerning the manner in which it should act upon such opinions as it might be able to form without such freedom. It differed from the English Bill of Rights in recognizing that the source of danger was not a sovereign on a throne but a majority in legislative chambers. Like the English Bill, however, it said nothing about a freedom from fear, meaning security against the danger of foreign aggression, nor about a freedom from want, meaning security against the consequences of misfortune in the pursuit of food, clothing, and shelter. Such matters were left to the care of those who had the power to determine the policies of the government. The framers of these bills of rights were more concerned with the processes of government than with its policies in matters of defense and welfare. The important difference between these two famous bills of rights consisted in the method of dealing with the problem of enforcement. The English revolutionists relied mainly upon the good will and the good sense of their Parliament. The Americans, who framed the Constitution of the new and more powerful Union, relied not only on their congressmen but also, to a greater degree than in England, on their judges.

The most thoughtful of the American political leaders at the time of the adoption of the Constitution were by no means agreed concerning the practical importance of a federal bill of rights. James Madison, who was a member of the First Congress under the Constitution as well as of the Federal Convention, and took the lead in framing the first ten amendments, set no great store by what they might accomplish. Writing to Thomas Jefferson October 17, 1788, he gave four reasons for attaching little importance to a federal bill of rights.[10] The first was that, since the Federal Government would possess no powers except those granted by the Constitution, it would be less likely to abuse its authority than state governments possessing undefined and,

37

therefore, largely unlimited powers. His second reason was that he feared agreement could not be obtained on definitions of some essential rights as broad as he would deem desirable. He mentioned particularly the freedom of conscience which the people of some states were not prepared to define as broadly as Virginia had recently done in its statute of religious freedom. Thirdly, the nature of the federal system itself, he thought, afforded a safeguard against the abuse of power by the Federal Government, which did not exist in the case of the unitary governments of the states. Finally, he wrote: "Experience proves the inefficacy of the bills of rights on occasions when it is most needed. Repeated violations of these parchment barriers," he declared, "have been committed by overbearing majorities in every state."

Nevertheless, Madison was of the opinion that a federal bill of rights might be of some practical value. His letter to Jefferson made it clear that Madison was more afraid of the abuse of power by the legislative branch of the government than by the executive. The source of fear in 1788 was very different from that a century earlier in England. It was not the tyranny of kings but of parliaments against which safeguards were then needed. "Wherever the real power of Government lies," he wrote, "there is the danger of oppression. In our government the real power lies in the majority of the community, and the invasion of private rights is to be apprehended chiefly, not from acts of Government contrary to the sense of its constituents, but from acts in which the Government is the mere instrument of the major number of constituents." Madison continued, "What use, it may be asked, can a bill of rights serve in popular governments? I answer, the two following, which, though less essential than in other governments, sufficiently recommend the precaution: (1) The political truths declared in that solemn manner acquire by degrees the character of fundamental maxims of free government and, as they become incorporated with the national sentiment, counteract the impulses of interest and passion. (2) Although it be generally true, as above stated, that the danger of oppression lies in the interested majorities of the people rather than in usurped acts of the government, yet there may be occasions on which the evil may spring from the latter source; and on such, a bill of rights will be a good ground for an appeal to the sense of the community." It should be noted well that Madison failed to mention the safeguarding of popular rights by judicial proceedings of any kind. He was still thinking, as were the framers of the original state bills of rights, of the educational value of general principles of government and of good advice to the people, when impressively set forth in solemn state papers.

Jefferson, who was still in Paris, did not reply to Madison's letter until March 15, 1789. He then addressed himself to Madison's irresolute defense of a federal bill of rights and emphasized the important argument that Madison had neglected.[11] "In the arguments in favor of a declaration of rights," Jefferson wrote, "you omit one which has great weight with me; the legal check which it puts into the hands of the judiciary. This is a body," he added, "which, rendered independent and kept strictly to its own department, merits great confidence for its learning and integrity." Jefferson took up one by one Madison's four reasons for setting little store by a federal bill of rights, giving his own reasons for setting greater store by such a bill. He conceded that a declaration of rights is, as he put it, "like all other human blessings alloyed with some inconveniences" and not likely to accomplish fully its object, but he was convinced that the good results would outweigh the evil. It is clear what he felt those good results would be. They would be the consequences of the greater security for essential human rights and fundamental freedoms through the added opportunity to supplement appeals to public opinion by appeals to the judges in the courts of law.

Another one of the most thoughtful political leaders of the time, Alexander Hamilton, had very different ideas from

39

those of Jefferson. In No. 84 of the *Federalist Papers* Hamilton set forth his views concerning the desirability of a federal bill of rights.[12] He was replying to the critics of the Constitution, as submitted to the states for ratification, who deplored the absence of a federal bill of rights. Hamilton remarked that bills of rights were originally stipulations between kings and their subjects, that they constituted abridgments of the royal prerogative in furtherance of the privileges of Parliament, and that they were not much concerned with the reservation of rights to the people at large. The history of the English Revolution of 1688 was familiar enough to his readers, and he did not need to enlarge on that subject. Referring to the purposes of the people in adopting a federal Constitution, as stated in the Preamble, he declared that this Preamble was of greater value to the people than a detailed enumeration of general principles of government or any amount of good advice to politicians. "Here is a better recognition of popular rights," he asserted, "than volumes of those aphorisms which make the principal figure in several of our state bills of rights, and which would sound much better in a treatise of ethics than in a constitution of government."

Hamilton understood as well as Jefferson the importance of the services that might be rendered by independent judges of learning and integrity. In No. 78 of the *Federalist Papers* he set forth the classic exposition of the doctrine of judicial review and propounded the theory of the judicial veto. With this part of Hamilton's argument there would have been no dissent on the part of either Madison or Jefferson. In No. 81 of the *Federalist Papers* Hamilton set forth his views concerning the manner in which an independent Supreme Court might employ its powers of judicial review and veto. This is the point at which Jefferson, at least, would have parted company from Hamilton.

This part of Hamilton's argument was addressed to the popular objection against the proposed Constitution that the judges would be able to interpret the spirit as well as

the letter of the Constitution and thereby be able to determine the policy of legislative measures. Hamilton recognized the danger of this objection to the proposed federal
Constitution by friends of popular government who feared
that the government under the new Constitution might get
out of control by the people. He did not make his own view
as clear as he might have done, if he could have been sure
that his views would have met with popular approval, but
the implication of his argument is plain. Hamilton hoped
that an independent Supreme Court, able to put popular
measures sponsored by the people's representatives to the
test of compliance with the spirit of the Constitution as
interpreted by the judges, would succeed in giving the whole
system of constitutional government a more aristocratic
character than would be pleasing to the friends of a genuine
government of the people. He did not share Jefferson's
interest in a federal bill of rights that would make the
Supreme Court a more potent guardian of basic human
rights and fundamental freedoms. His belief was that a
powerful Supreme Court would constitute a more effective
guardian of the vested interests of property owners without
a bill of rights than with one.

This conflict between the Hamiltonian and Jeffersonian
views concerning the proper function of the Supreme Court
in interpreting the constitutional rights of Americans supplies an important clue to the controversial role of the
Supreme Court in United States history. Both these concepts
of the doctrine of judicial review imply the existence of a
power somewhere to read the spirit of the fundamental law
into the language of the written Constitution. Presumably
the people of the United States possessed the right to breathe
the spirit of American life into the Constitution, but this
right of the people was dependent in practice upon the power
of public opinion, and that power in turn was contingent not
only upon the nature of the civic education but also upon the
practical efficacy of the constitutional freedom of the press

4

and the other freedoms that are essential to the development and expression of public opinion. The people of the Revolution put their confidence for the preservation of the revolutionary spirit largely in their representatives in the state legislatures and in the little samples of the public serving on the juries. This confidence was not misplaced as long as the problem of protecting the people against the abuse of governmental power was merely a question of protecting those interests that were popular. But for the protection of unpopular interests, those concerned would have to look to the judges. Judges after all are also people, and may be expected, because of their professional training and special experience in public affairs and greater security of tenure, to maintain a better balance than other kinds of public officers between the temporary interest of the public in doing what they please and their permanent interest in behaving as they ought under the Constitution. Nevertheless, whether judges were in fact Hamiltonians or Jeffersonians was bound to make a great deal of difference in the adaptation of the Constitution to the various crises of human affairs in the years ahead.

The American Bill of Rights is often considered to be identical with the first ten amendments to the federal Constitution; that is, the federal Bill of Rights. In fact, this is only a part of the constitutional provision for protecting the fundamental freedoms of Americans. The various bills of rights adopted along with the original state constitutions also formed a part of the whole body of basic human rights and fundamental freedoms, claimed by Americans in the period of the Revolution. The state bills of rights, as we have seen, derived their practical force mainly from the good opinion of them held by the people of the several states. The ultimate sanction for their enforcement was educational rather than political or judicial. The practical efficacy of such sanctions depended upon the nature of the educational systems in different states and on the effects of such educational systems on public opinion, state by state. The practical efficacy of the federal Bill of Rights depended more largely upon the opinion of judges and on what it was possible to achieve in the course of litigation in the courts of law. To a lesser extent the reliance for enforcement of the federal Bill of Rights was placed upon the power of public opinion sustained by the whole body of the American people.

The importance of federal judges and of national public opinion in promoting respect for and observance of fundamental freedoms cannot be estimated without reference to the nature of the Federal Union and the relations between the governments of its component parts and the government of the whole. In the beginning the federal judges were responsible only for the enforcement of the supremacy of the federal Bill of Rights over ordinary acts of Congress.[13] Neither they nor the whole body of the American people could dictate to the people of a particular state concerning the rights of individuals under the constitution of that state. It was customary to speak of the states at that time as sovereign states. Certainly the people of each of them would have insisted on promoting respect for fundamental freedoms in accordance with their own particular notions concerning the nature of essential human rights. This might lead, and in fact did lead, to the existence side by side in different states of very different ideas concerning the rights of men and of citizens.

The sensational Dred Scott Case offered the conclusive evidence of the original uncertainty concerning the nature of the fundamental freedoms of Americans.[14] Chief Justice Taney expressed the opinion that the descendants of African slaves, whether freed or held in bondage, were not and could not become citizens of the United States. He added that it was the general opinion at the time of the Revolution that Negroes had no rights which the white inhabitants of the country were bound to respect. Justice Curtis, in an

43

opinion in the same case which commands more approval today from students of constitutional law than it did in 1857 from his own colleagues on the Supreme Court, expressed the contrary view. Free Negroes, he argued, could become citizens and would be entitled to the same rights as the free white inhabitants of the country. But neither judicial decisions nor public discussion could create a uniform opinion concerning the rights of free Negroes under the Constitution as it stood at that time.

The role of federal judges in promoting respect for fundamental freedoms was profoundly changed by the Fourteenth Amendment to the federal Constitution. By this amendment the Supreme Court was charged with responsibility for putting the privileges and immunities of American citizens upon a uniform basis throughout the Union. The states were forbidden to make or enforce any law that should abridge the privileges or immunities of citizens of the United States; nor might they deprive any person of life, liberty, or property without due process of law; nor deny to any person within their jurisdictions the equal protection of the law. This expansion of the jurisdiction of the Supreme Court involved a degree of interference in the internal affairs of the different states that would have been abhorrent to most of the original framers of the American Constitution. It ensured an end to such differences of opinion concerning fundamental freedoms as had been disclosed by the Dred Scott Case. It opened a new era for the action of public opinion, as well as of federal judges, in promoting respect for basic human rights.

An international declaration or bill of rights, however, if promulgated by authority of the United Nations, would not stand on the same basis as the federal Bill of Rights, either before or after the adoption of the Fourteenth Amendment. It would stand more nearly on the basis of what might have passed for a federal bill of rights under the original frame of government for the United States, that is, the Articles of Confederation. Under these articles there was neither a bill of rights nor an independent judiciary. The nearest approach to a formal statement of the fundamental freedoms of Americans was the Declaration of Independence. This was comprehensive and emphatic, but did not provide clear guidance to judges. A claim to an inalienable right to pursue happiness may afford much aid and comfort to an embattled people struggling against what they believe to be tyrannical oppression. It actually furnished an important link in the chain of arguments in support of a lawful right of revolution.

But after revolution comes the need for ordered liberty and civil rights. The Articles of Confederation did not attempt to define the privileges and immunities of citizens of the United States, though they did provide that the free inhabitants of each state should be entitled to all privileges and immunities of free citizens in the several states.[15] It also provided that the people of each state should enjoy the right of free migration among the states and free participation in the privileges of trade and commerce without discrimination on account of their residence in any particular state. These special privileges of American citizenship were designed the better to secure and perpetuate mutual friendship and intercourse among the people of the different states in the Confederation. Years later Chief Justice Taney was to show how uncertain and unequal these privileges might be even under the Constitution of the new and more perfect Union. But in the beginning protection for the rights of Americans was to be found mainly in the dependence of the government of the Confederation upon the governments of the states and in the force, particularly the educational force, of the state bills of rights.

So, presumably, it will be with the promotion of respect for basic human rights and fundamental freedoms by the United Nations. Nevertheless, the experience of the American people in promoting respect for and observance of civil rights under the Constitution of the United States should not be without value to the peoples of the United Nations. The privileges and immunities of citizens of the United States are, in fact, something more than the privileges and immunities of citizens of the several states, and so it should be also under the Charter of the United Nations.

The Constitutional Privileges and Immunities of Americans

THE constitutional privileges and immunities of Americans must be deduced from the general principles of free government, the good advice, and the explicit limitations upon the powers and procedures of the federal and state governments set forth in the original declarations and bills of rights, and revised and enlarged by successive constitutional changes. It is evident that in the last analysis the security for these rights rests upon the favorable opinion of the people. The opinions of lawmakers, of law-enforcement officers, and particularly of judges may be of exceptional importance in the actual process of making these rights secure, but the ultimate source of their opinions is the general body of public opinion. It cannot be expected that the stream will rise higher than the source. Those who wish to promote respect for basic human rights among the peoples of the United Nations will be interested in observing the extent to which the constitutional rights of Americans are actually secured at the present time, and in appraising the relative importance of judicial processes and of general civic education in giving effective sanction to the fundamental freedoms of Americans.

Since the end of World War II and the unprecedented growth of world-wide interest in basic human rights, there has begun a period of self-examination by the American people with a view toward a better understanding of their own privileges and immunities. The various organizations that conduct polls of public opinion, the Hutchins Commis-

The Notes to this lecture begin on page 153.

sion on the Freedom of the Press, sponsored by Time Incorporated, and above all the President's Committee on Civil Rights under the chairmanship of Mr. Charles E. Wilson, have contributed to an unparalleled amount of introspection by the American people. They have disclosed growing awareness of a wide gap between the privileges and immunities of citizens, as set forth in state papers, and the actual participation in their enjoyment by various kinds and classes of people in the United States. The record shows that a great deal has been accomplished to realize the vision of those American revolutionists who framed the original declarations and bills of rights. It also shows that a great deal remains to be accomplished.

Let us look first at the record as disclosed by the pollsters. On September 22, 1945, the American Institute of Public Opinion [1] published the answers to this question: "Do you favor or oppose a law in your state which would require employers to hire a person if he is qualified for the job regardless of his race or color?" Of those to whom the question was put, 13 per cent expressed no opinion; 43 per cent were in favor of such a law; and 44 per cent were opposed. The returns for the country as a whole seemed to show a remarkably equal division of opinion. A breakdown of the returns by sections, however, showed that opinions were apparently influenced much more by local circumstances than by national traditions. In New England and the Middle Atlantic states 58 per cent of those who responded favored such a law and 31 per cent opposed it. In the South only 30 per cent favored such a law and 60 per cent opposed it. It might be supposed that a long-standing declaration of national faith in equal rights regardless of racial differences would have produced general agreement in favor of such a law, but in fact no such agreement was found and in certain regions the prospect of such an agreement seemed remote.

On June 2, 1946, the National Opinion Research Center [2] published the answers to another significant question: "In peacetime, do you think that newspapers should be allowed to criticize our form of government?" Of the poll, 64 per cent said yes, an answer that seems to be clearly required by the American tradition, but 5 per cent were undecided, and 31 per cent said definitely no. This is a surprising amount of dissent to a proposition that would seem to be clearly implied by a genuine belief in the freedom of the press. On July 4 of the same year the same organization published [3] the answers to two other significant questions: (1) "In peacetime, do you think people in this country should be allowed to say anything they want to in a public speech?" This question perhaps leaves too much to the imagination, since there are obviously some things, such as direct and dangerously persuasive incitement to lawlessness and criminal violence, which are surely not covered by the traditional American claim to freedom of speech, but presumably the pollsters made clear that their question related to the essentialities of the principle. Be that as it may, 64 per cent of the answers were in the affirmative, 32 per cent were in the negative, and 4 per cent were undecided. At the same time the National Opinion Research Center asked: "In peacetime, do you think members of the Communist party should be allowed to speak on the radio?" To this question only 49 per cent answered yes, while 39 per cent answered no, and 12 per cent were undecided. Evidently many persons either did not believe that Communists were people or did not believe that freedom of speech applied to speaking over the air in the same way as to a visible audience.

The pollsters themselves perhaps were puzzled by these answers and began to wonder just what the Bill of Rights meant to the American people. On October 6, 1946, the National Opinion Research Center [4] published the answers to these questions: "What do you know about the Bill of Rights? Do you know anything it says? Have you ever heard of it?" Of those who were interviewed, 31 per cent admitted that they had never heard of the Bill of Rights or were not sure what it was; 36 per cent claimed to have

49

heard of it, but could not identify it; 12 per cent thought they could identify it, but gave incorrect, confused, or otherwise unsatisfactory answers. Only 21 per cent gave reasonably accurate answers. The proportion of satisfactory answers varied widely among different classes of people and in different sections of the country. It was twice as high in the West as in the South. It was three times as high among professional people as among manual workers and employees in factories. Satisfactory answers were obtained from 41 per cent of those who had attended college, but from only 8 per cent of those whose education had not gone beyond the eighth grade.

Assuming that these answers offer a reliable index of the state of mind concerning the contents of the early American declarations and bills of rights, it is not surprising that there should be much to be desired in the actual enjoyment of these rights by the various kinds and classes of people in the United States. That such is in fact the prevalent opinion was disclosed by a more recent poll conducted by the *Fortune* survey directed by Elmo Roper.[5] Mr. Roper's question to his selected sample of the American people was as follows: "Opinions differ as to how certain racial and religious groups are treated in this country. Which of these ideas comes closest to expressing your opinion of what the real situation is?" Mr. Roper's findings were published in *Fortune* magazine for October 1947. Of the total number of answers, 25 per cent affirmed that racial and religious groups in this country are on the whole as well treated as they should be; 36 per cent were of the opinion that, while certain racial and religious groups in this country are sometimes not treated as well as they should be, we are now improving the situation as fast as is practical; 28 per cent agreed that certain racial and religious groups in this country are treated very badly, and that some strong measures should be taken to improve the situation; 11 per cent expressed no opinion. The important group here, as Mr. Roper pointed out in his published comment on the poll, is the 28 per cent who favor strong measures to correct existing wrongs. This group is made up of approximately twenty-two million adults, all of whom would support changes in the direction of greater tolerance, and many of whom might actively participate in bringing such changes about. His opinion was that this group represents the main hope of the members of the racial and religious groups, which are the victims of discrimination, for a wider participation in the enjoyment of the basic human rights and fundamental freedoms which the framers of the revolutionary declarations and bills sought to establish.

In view of the uncertainties and differences of opinion concerning the nature and content and implications of the American declarations and bills of rights, it is not surprising that there should be much contemporary controversy concerning the meaning of Americanism. What are we to think of the methods of the Committee on Un-American Activities of the House of Representatives at Washington, of the processes employed for purging the Department of State and other executive departments and establishments of the Government of the United States of allegedly disloyal employees, of the legislation prohibiting the expression of political opinions in the official publications of trade-unions, of the legislation designed to force trade-unions to discriminate against the members of a certain political party in the elections of their officers, and of the official efforts to force private employers to discriminate against certain classes of persons in their employment regardless of their guilt or innocence of offenses under the laws of the land? What are we to think also of the judicial enforcement of land covenants discriminating against the members of certain races? [5a] What are we to think of the political controversy over the fair-employment practices bill, the antilynching and antipoll-tax bills, and other measures designed to secure equality of treatment for Negroes? The educational process, set in motion by the Declaration of Independence, seems to have accomplished less than it should in 172 years.

Where public opinion is so uncertain, or perplexed, or confused, Americans have been accustomed to rely upon the courts for the interpretation and protection of their rights. Where public opinion gives a clear answer in line with the American traditions, there is, as a rule, no occasion for an appeal to the courts. But where a majority appears to be out of line with the traditions, and their representatives in legislative bodies or on trial juries fail to respect claims to fundamental freedoms based upon the revolutionary declarations and bills of rights, the judges have the opportunity to speak the sober second thoughts of the American people. The interesting question arises: Has judicial opinion offered greater security for fundamental freedoms than public opinion?

The record of judicial enforcement of basic human rights and fundamental freedoms falls into three parts. First, there is the attempt at judicial enforcement of the spirit of the Constitution. Secondly, there is the record of judicial enforcement of substantive constitutional limitations on governmental power. Thirdly, there is the record of judicial enforcement of procedural limitations on governmental power. The record of the courts in promoting respect for and observance of fundamental freedoms will be examined under these three heads.

It has often been argued that the courts should not try to enforce the spirit of the Constitution, but should confine their attention to the letter of that document. This is the view commonly expressed by the leading authorities on constitutional law.[6] This, however, as we have already observed, was not the opinion of such earlier authorities as Thomas Jefferson and Alexander Hamilton. These two eminent statesmen disagreed radically concerning the kind of spirit they would like to see read into the Constitution, but each was apparently disposed, when the ratification of the Constitution was the main question before the people of the United States, to have faith in the practical capacity of the judges to make a constructive use of the power of

52

judicial review. Prior to the adoption of the Fourteenth Amendment, except for the regrettable prosecutions under the Sedition Act of 1798, there were few cases in which an opportunity to promote respect for basic human rights was presented to the federal courts. Subsequently, such cases became comparatively numerous.

An early case of this sort grew out of Dorr's Rebellion in Rhode Island more than one hundred years ago.[7] The federal Constitution guarantees to the people of the states a republican form of government. Dorr's Rebellion climaxed a long and bitterly contested struggle to supplant an antiquated state constitution, which reserved special privileges to property owners, by a constitution designed to establish a more popular form of government. The Supreme Court evaded the issue in this case, holding that it was a political question which did not present an issue suitable for decision in a court of law. A genuinely Jeffersonian court, however, might have found a way to do something to promote greater respect for basic human rights. A more important case was that of Dred Scott.[8] In this case the Supreme Court went out of its way to try to settle an issue which most Americans regarded as political. Unfortunately, it tried to settle this issue by putting the rights of property owners above the rights of man. The result of this misguided effort should have constituted a sufficient warning to judges who might be tempted to put the Hamiltonian concept of the spirit of the Constitution above the Jeffersonian.

In recent years the most significant cases affording an opportunity for the Supreme Court to apply the spirit of the Constitution arose in connection with applications for naturalization by persons who wished to become American citizens, while reserving to themselves the right not to fight in any war to which they might have conscientious objections. The first of these cases, decided in 1929, was that of Madame Rosika Schwimmer,[9] who was opposed on principle to fighting in any war, believing that all wars were wrong. The majority of the Court denied her the right of naturalization under an act of Congress requiring that candidates for citizenship should be willing to defend the Constitution and laws of the United States against all enemies. Madame Schwimmer, though willing to take the prescribed oath, declared that she would not take up arms personally, being "an uncompromising pacifist." There was, in fact, little likelihood that a woman of her age, or even a man of her age, would be called upon to bear arms in defense of the country, but a majority of the Court considered that an important principle was at stake. They contended that such a pacifist could not be a good American. The Naturalization Act of 1906 was admittedly ambiguous on this point, but the majority of the judges evidently were of the opinion that, whatever exceptions might be allowable for native-born pacifists, it was not the intention of the Congress to waive the obligation to defend the Constitution by arms, if necessary, for aliens seeking to become citizens.

Justice Holmes, with whom Justices Brandeis and Sanford agreed, protested stoutly against this decision. He seized the opportunity to reiterate some good advice, such as presumably would have been approved by the framers of the revolutionary declarations and bills of rights. "Surely it can not show lack of attachment to the principles of the Constitution," he wrote, "that she thinks it can be improved. I suppose that most intelligent people think that it might be. Her particular improvement looking to the abolition of war seems to me not materially different in the bearing on this case from a wish to establish a cabinet government as in England, or a single house, or one term of seven years for the President." Justice Holmes then turned his attention from good advice to fundamental principles of government. "Some of her answers might excite popular prejudice, but if there is any principle of the Constitution that more imperatively calls for attachment than any other it is the principle of free thought—not free thought for those who agree with us but freedom for the thought that we hate." But Justice Holmes's argument that the members of Congress must be presumed to share the liberal spirit of the framers of the revolutionary declarations and bills of rights fell on deaf ears. A majority of his colleagues obdurately refused to ascribe to the authors of the Naturalization Act a greater degree of liberality than they had plainly expressed in the actual words of the statute.

The same issue arose shortly afterwards in the case of Douglas Macintosh,[10] a professor of theology in the Yale Divinity School and a man who had made a glorious record under fire in World War I as a chaplain of a Canadian regiment. Professor Macintosh, unlike Madame Schwimmer, was willing to fight for his country in a just war, but not in a war that he considered unjust. This mental reservation prevented him from taking the oath of allegiance in a form acceptable to the Court of Naturalization, and his case, like that of Madame Schwimmer, eventually reached the Supreme Court of the United States. Again the Court found him ineligible under the statute. Justice Sutherland, speaking for a bare majority of the judges, disposed of Professor Macintosh's conscientious scruples by observing that: "We are a nation . . . . whose government must go forward on the assumption that unqualified allegiance to the nation and submission and obedience to the laws of the land, as well those made for war as those made for peace, are not inconsistent with the will of God."

In this case Chief Justice Hughes wrote the opinion for the dissenting justices. He sought to put their objections to the exclusion of Professor Macintosh from citizenship on new and firmer ground. "There is abundant room for enforcing the requisite authority of the law," the Chief Justice declared, "without demanding that either citizens or applicants for citizenship shall assume by oath an obligation to regard allegiance to God as subordinate to allegiance to civil power." Chief Justice Hughes supported his opinion by an appeal to a higher law than that embodied in any ordinary statute or even in the Constitution itself. "Much has been said," he wrote, "of the paramount duty to the

state, a duty to be recognized, it is urged, even though it
conflicts with convictions of duty to God. Undoubtedly that
duty to the state exists within the domain of power, for
government may enforce obedience to law regardless of
scruples. When one's belief collides with the power of the
state the latter is supreme within its sphere and submission
or punishment follows. But, in the forum of conscience, duty
to a moral power higher than the state has always been
maintained. Preservation of that supreme obligation, as a
matter of principle, would unquestionably be made by many
of our conscientious and law-abiding citizens. The essence
of religion is belief in a relation to God involving duties
superior to those arising from any human relations. One can
not speak of religious liberty, with proper appreciation of
its essential and historical significance, without assuming
the existence of a belief in supreme allegiance to the will of
God."

Chief Justice Hughes's appeal to a higher law as a guide
to the nature of fundamental freedoms to be enjoyed by
applicants for citizenship, as well as by citizens, did not
prevent the majority of the Court from sanctioning the exclusion of Professor Macintosh, but the decision continued
to weigh on the consciences of the dissenting judges. It also
weighed on the consciences of some of the new members of
the Court, until fifteen years later an opportunity for recon-
sideration was afforded by another case involving an application for citizenship by a conscientious objector. This time
the applicant was a Seventh-Day Adventist, by name
Girouard.[11] The precedents, set up in the Schwimmer and
Macintosh cases, were at last found to be unworthy of the
American tradition of respect for basic human rights and
fundamental freedoms. They were overruled, and the principle was established that the spirit of the framers of the
revolutionary declarations and bills of rights is to be presumed to animate the makers of laws under the Constitution,
where the letter of the law is susceptible of such an interpretation. This decision was a splendid triumph for the Jeffer-

sonian version of judicial power. It was not reached, however, until the year 1946, 155 years after the ratification
of the federal Bill of Rights.

The record of judicial enforcement of substantive limitations on governmental power is longer and more impressive. It might be supposed that the most important
source of judicial power to protect the basic human rights
and fundamental freedoms of Americans would be the constitutional provisions designed to safeguard the privileges
and immunities of citizens. In the original Constitution there
was an explicit provision that the citizens of each state
should be entitled to all the privileges and immunities of
citizens in the several states. The Fourteenth Amendment
added the further provision that no state should make or
enforce any law abridging the privileges and immunities of
citizens of the United States. Nothing was said concerning
the abridgment of such privileges and immunities by private
persons or organized bodies of any kind other than the governments of states. The extent of the responsibility for safeguarding basic human rights imposed upon the Supreme
Court by these provisions was not altogether clear. It might
seem, however, that these provisions of the Constitution
would have become the basis for much positive action by
the Supreme Court. In fact, there have been few cases in
which the Supreme Court has been called upon to consider
action under these clauses and astonishingly little has actually
been done by the Court under the authority presumably conferred upon it by them.

The first case involving the privileges and immunities of
citizens reached the Court shortly before the ratification of
the Fourteenth Amendment. This was the case of *Crandall*
v. *Nevada*.[12] It involved a law of that state imposing a tax
of one dollar on every person leaving the state by railroad,
stagecoach, or other commercial conveyance. This case
might have been disposed of on the ground of an unconstitutional interference with the regulation of interstate
commerce, but a majority of the Court were of the opinion

that the free movement of citizens of the United States from one point to another within the Union, particularly to the Capitol and to other places where agencies of the Federal Government might be found, was one of the privileges of federal citizenship and was not to be interfered with by state tax laws. But when a few years later an attempt was made in the Slaughter House Cases [13] to extend the privileges and immunities of United States citizens to include a general freedom of business enterprise, a majority of the Court said that the Fourteenth Amendment was not to be construed as having accomplished such a result. Civil rights, according to Justice Miller, who wrote the opinion for the Court in these cases as well as in the earlier case of *Crandall* v. *Nevada,* were partly federal and partly state, and the part under the guardianship of state laws and state judges was still much the larger part.

In recent years there have been several interesting cases in which similar claims were raised. Up to now, however, such claims have always been raised without success. One interesting case was that involving Mayor Hague of Jersey City and the C.I.O.,[14] decided in 1939. The C.I.O. sought through its organizers to hold public meetings in city parks for the discussion of matters in which workers might be interested, particularly matters of organization under the National Labor Relations Act. Mayor Hague claimed a right to prevent such meetings, regardless of the purposes for which they might be called, on the ground that they might lead to disorder and disturbance of the peace. The labor organizers contended that the chances of uncontrollable disorder were small and that under the circumstances it was the duty of the police to protect such meetings rather than to disperse them. A majority of the Supreme Court were of the same opinion but were unable to agree upon the reasons for their opinion. Two of the judges, Justices Roberts and Black, believed that Mayor Hague's refusal to give adequate protection to such meetings deprived the citizens who wished to attend of privileges and immunities guaranteed by the Constitution, but other members of the Court found technical reasons for disposing of the case on other grounds. Chief Justice Hughes wrote in a separate opinion that he believed the right to discuss the National Labor Relations Act in public was a privilege of a citizen of the United States, though he was not satisfied that the Court could dispose of that particular case on that ground. The other judges did not even recognize such a privilege of citizenship. The decision of the Court, while favorable to the freedom of labor organizers to assemble and hold meetings in such cases, left the public at large as uncertain as before concerning the privileges and immunities of United States citizenship.

Another case, in which the same question arose, was that of *Edwards* v. *California*,[15] decided in 1941. In this case Edwards, a resident of California, brought his brother-in-law, Duncan by name, from Texas, where he was having difficulty in earning a living, to his own state to make a fresh start in life. There Duncan presently sought relief from the public authorities. The California legislature had passed an act prohibiting the transport into that state of persons likely to become public charges, and the question arose whether Edwards could properly be punished for bringing in such a person. The Supreme Court decided unanimously that California had no right to make such a law, but there was wide difference of opinion within the Court concerning the reasons for the decision. Five of the judges, constituting a bare majority of the Court, were of the opinion that the California statute trespassed upon the authority of Congress to regulate interstate commerce, and that, since Congress had made no law regulating the transportation of indigent persons among the states, presumably such transportation was to remain unrestricted.

The other members of the Court could not agree that the transportation of indigent persons in relatives' automobiles was to be treated like the transportation of cattle, fruit, steel, or coal. Justice Douglas argued forcefully that the right of Americans to move freely from state to state occupies a more protected position in our governmental system than the movement of cattle across state lines. It was, in short, a right of national citizenship guaranteed against interference on the part of the states by the privileges and immunities of citizenship clause. Justice Jackson felt strongly on the subject and wrote a separate opinion to give adequate expression to his views. "Does indigence," he indignantly inquired, "constitute a basis for restricting the freedom of a citizen, as crime or contagion warrants its restriction? We should say now, and in no uncertain terms, that a man's mere property status, without more, cannot be used by a state to test, qualify, or limit his rights as a citizen of the United States. . . . . I think California had no right to make the condition of Duncan's purse . . . . the basis of excluding him or punishing one who extended him aid."

Justice Jackson's further comments on this case form one of the most eloquent passages in the recent opinions of the members of the Supreme Court. "If I doubted whether his federal citizenship alone were enough to open the gates of California to Duncan," he wrote, "my doubt would disappear on consideration of the obligations of such citizenship. Duncan owes a duty to render military service, and this Court has said that this duty is the result of his citizenship. . . . . A contention that a citizen's duty to render military service is suspended by 'indigence' would meet with little favor. Rich or penniless, Duncan's citizenship under the Constitution pledges his strength to the defense of California as a part of the United States, and his right to migrate to any part of the land he must defend is something she must respect under the same instrument. Unless this Court is willing to say that citizenship of the United States means at least this much to the citizen, then our heritage of constitutional privileges and immunities is only a promise to the ear to be broken to the hope, a teasing illusion like a munificent bequest in a pauper's will." But in this case, as in that of *Mayor Hague* v. *C.I.O.*, the majority of the Court rejected the good advice of the spokesmen for the minority and insisted on disposing of the case on grounds other than those afforded by the clause of the Constitution that guarantees the privileges and immunities of citizens of the United States.

Those judges of the Supreme Court who believed that the privileges and immunities of citizenship mean something and should receive better protection from the Court refused to accept defeat. The most recent case in which they have contended for judicial enforcement of civil rights based upon this clause of the Constitution is that of *Adamson* v. *California*,[16] decided in June 1947. This case involved a claim by a citizen, convicted of murder in the state of California, that he had been wrongly compelled to give testimony against himself in consequence of rulings by the trial judge concerning the admissibility of certain evidence against him. Justice Black seized the opportunity to discuss the whole record of the Supreme Court in interpreting the clause of the Constitution relating to the privileges and immunities of citizens. He contended strenuously that the framers of the Fourteenth Amendment had intended to protect not only the equal rights of the freedmen in the former slave states but also the rights of citizens of every description to the enjoyment of all the privileges and immunities mentioned in the federal Bill of Rights against abridgment by the state governments as well as by that of the United States. Justices Douglas, Murphy, and Rutledge agreed with him that the specific guarantees of the federal Bill of Rights should be read into the first paragraph of the Fourteenth Amendment, guaranteeing the privileges and immunities of citizens of the United States against abridgment by any act of a state. But the majority refused to accept this view and the position of the Supreme Court, restricting the privileges and immunities of United States citizenship to a narrow list of civil rights, relating to specific relations with the

Federal Government such as the right to travel to the national capital, remains unchanged.

The Supreme Court has been somewhat more successful in enforcing those substantive limitations on governmental power that are clearly expressed in the Constitution. For example, both Congress and the states are expressly forbidden to pass any bill of attainder or ex post facto law, and the states are also forbidden to pass any law impairing the obligation of a contract. As early as 1810 the Supreme Court in the case of *Fletcher* v. *Peck* [17] decided that this provision prevented the legislature of Georgia from rescinding a grant of land to certain parties, although the parties had originally obtained the grant by bribery. The guilty were to be punished, if punishable at all, by proper proceedings in a criminal court, not by a subsequent act of the legislature voiding titles to land acquired under the original grant. Chief Justice Marshall in the course of his opinion made some significant remarks about the constitutional rights of Americans. "Whatever respect might have been felt for the state sovereignties," he wrote, "it is not to be disguised that the framers of the Constitution viewed, with some apprehension, the violent acts which might grow out of the feelings of the moment; and that the people of the United States, in adopting that instrument, have manifested a determination to shield themselves and their property from the effects of those sudden and strong passions to which men are exposed. The restrictions on the legislative power of the States are obviously founded in this sentiment; and the Constitution of the United States contains what may be deemed a bill of rights for the people of each State." The conclusion of the Court was unanimous. In Marshall's words: "The State of Georgia was restrained, either by general principles which are common to our free institutions, or by the particular provisions of the Constitution of the United States, from passing a law" such as that in question in this case. In this decision both the Federalist judges and the Jeffersonians concurred.

That the decision in *Fletcher* v. *Peck* was more Hamiltonian than Jeffersonian is not debatable. Nor can there be doubt of the Jeffersonian character of the latest Supreme Court decision under these clauses of the Constitution in the cases of Lovett and others versus the United States.[18] In these cases, brought by three civil officers of the Federal Government whose political opinions were displeasing to congressmen and who were consequently deprived of their salaries by an amendment to an appropriation bill, the Supreme Court had no difficulty in finding that such discrimination was in effect a bill of attainder. Justice Black, who delivered the opinion of the Court, put the judicial objections to such legislation in the strongest terms. "Section 304, thus, clearly accomplishes the punishment of named individuals without a judicial trial. The fact that the punishment is inflicted through the instrumentality of an Act specifically cutting off the pay of certain named individuals, found guilty of disloyalty, makes it no less galling or effective than if it had been done by an Act which designated the conduct as criminal. No one would think that Congress could have passed a valid law, stating that after investigation it had found Lovett, Dodd, and Watson 'guilty' of the crime of engaging in 'subversive activities,' defined that term for the first time, and sentenced them to perpetual exclusion from any government employment. Section 304, while it does not use that language, accomplished that result. The effect was to inflict punishment without the safeguards of a judicial trial and 'determined by no previous law or fixed rule.' The Constitution declares that that can not be done either by a state or by the United States."

Justice Black then passed from giving good advice to expounding one of the essential principles of American government. "Those who wrote our Constitution," he declared, "well knew the danger inherent in special legislative acts which take away the life, liberty, or property of particular named persons, because the legislature thinks them guilty of conduct which deserves punishment. They intended to safeguard the people of this country from punishment without trial by duly constituted courts. . . . . When our Constitution and Bill of Rights were written, our ancestors had ample reason to know that legislative trials and punishments were too dangerous to liberty to exist in the nation of free men they envisioned. And so they proscribed bills of attainder. Much as we regret to declare that an Act of Congress violates the Constitution we have no alternative here." This decision was a splendid vindication of the constitutional immunity against bills of attainder, but, like the naturalization of conscientious objectors, it did not come until more than a century and a half after the adoption of the Constitution.

In general, the Supreme Court has not added much to the protection of basic human rights against abridgments by acts of Congress, which has been afforded by the general state of opinion among the people of the United States. This conclusion is most strikingly supported by the record of decisions in cases involving the power of Congress to protect Negroes against discrimination on account of their race or color. After the abolition of slavery, Congress adopted a variety of measures designed to secure the civil rights of freedmen and other Negroes, culminating in the Civil Rights Act of 1875. In a series of decisions the Supreme Court struck down the greater part of the safeguards which Congress sought to establish for the better protection of the Negroes' rights. These adverse decisions culminated in the case of *Butts* v. *Merchants and Miners Transportation Company*,[19] decided in 1913. In this case the Court held that even that part of the Civil Rights Act applicable to Negroes traveling from one state to another, and apparently clearly within the authority of Congress to enact under its power to regulate interstate commerce, should not be enforced. The theory of the Court was that, since the rest of the Act had been declared unconstitutional and local Jim Crow laws were recognized to be within the power of the states under the assumption that segregation, while involving racial distinctions, did not necessarily sanction racial discrimination, it was justified in assuming that Congress had not intended that this part of the measure should be enforced by itself alone. Congress showed no particular displeasure at this interpretation of its intentions, and public opinion seemed to sanction the attitude of the judges. It was not until 1946 that a majority of the Court finally reached the conclusion that a state Jim Crow law, applying to travel by bus from Washington to a point within the state of Virginia,[20] was an unconstitutional burden on interstate commerce. By then the evidence of the public-opinion polls showed that the Court was not in advance of the opinion of a majority of the people in most parts of the country.

The Supreme Court has been much more successful with the judicial enforcement of procedural limitations on governmental power. In the protection of strictly procedural rights indeed it has been at its best. There is a long record of decisions in which the Supreme Court has successfully maintained the rights of persons of most kinds to the benefit of the prescribed technicalities of due process of law. In recent years the New Deal Court has been particularly active in securing such rights for all classes of persons, particularly Negroes, in whose cases the Supreme Court for many years had seemed less effective than in protecting the rights of white people. The new and more effective attitude of the Supreme Court in cases concerning Negroes is well illustrated in a series of recent decisions. The opinion of Justice Black in the case of *Chambers* v. *Florida*,[21] decided in 1940, is particularly impressive. This case involved a Negro from whom a confession had been extorted by methods commonly known as the third degree employed in an extreme form. The facts in the case were clear and the Supreme Court refused to condone the abuse of third-degree methods on account of any alleged difficulties in procuring a conviction by lawful methods.

"We are not impressed," Justice Black wrote, "by the argument that law enforcement methods such as those under review are necessary to uphold our laws. The Constitution proscribes such lawless means irrespective of the end. And this argument flouts the basic principle that all people must stand on an equality before the bar of justice in every American court. Today as in ages past, we are not without tragic proof that the exalted power of some governments to punish manufactured crime dictatorially is the handmaid of tyranny. Under our constitutional system, courts stand against any winds that blow as havens of refuge for those who might otherwise suffer because they are helpless, weak, outnumbered, or because they are non-conforming victims of prejudice and public excitement. Due process of law, preserved for all by our Constitution, commands that no such practice as that disclosed by this record shall send any accused to his death. No higher duty, no more solemn responsibility, rests upon this Court, than that of translating into living law and maintaining this constitutional shield deliberately planned and inscribed for the benefit of every human being subject to our Constitution—of whatever race, creed or persuasion."

The Supreme Court has not been content, however, with an increasingly effective enforcement of the technical requirements of due process of law. It has read into that vague and difficult phrase a variety of meanings enabling it to play an active role in the determination of public policy, not only in Washington but also, by the adoption of the Fourteenth Amendment, at the state capitals. The great landmark in this development in the judicial enforcement of procedural limitations on governmental power was the New York bakers' ten-hour law case,[22] decided in 1905. In this case a majority of the Court denied the right of the legislature of the state of New York to limit the hours of labor in bakeshops on the ground that such a measure would deprive bakeshop proprietors as well as the employees of liberty without due process of law. By liberty the majority of the Court meant more than a mere immunity against restraints of the person. They included such novel liberties as a general freedom to make contracts concerning conditions of employment, regardless of the policies of state legislatures which might believe that restrictions upon the hours of labor were necessary and proper for the protection of the public health as well as the health of the workers directly concerned. The majority of the Court insisted upon giving effect to their own opinion concerning the reasonableness of such a measure, despite the protests of the other four judges. Justice Harlan wrote a vigorous and farsighted dissenting opinion, in which he warned against the danger of violating what he believed to be one of the fundamental principles of American government. This was that the reasonableness of legislation seeking to protect the public interest by imposing restrictions upon the activities of individuals should be determined by the elected representatives of the people rather than by judges, designed to be independent of political pressures, who could not be held directly responsible for the policies embodied in their decisions.

Justice Holmes, who was also one of the dissenting judges, wrote a separate opinion, which has become a famous landmark in the interpretation of the federal Bill of Rights. In this opinion he protested against giving the word "liberty" a philosophical interpretation unknown to the framers of the Constitution and not clearly sanctioned by contemporary public opinion. Despite these warnings the majority of the Supreme Court followed the precedent created in this case. In a long series of decisions the Court set aside a number of important federal statutes and a great quantity of state legislation embodying principles of public policy which the majority of the Court found objectionable. The tendency of these decisions was to protect the interests of property owners and managers of business corporations against regulation by laws enacted allegedly in the public interest. It is clear that the only logical basis of action under this novel interpretation of due process of law was afforded by the Hamiltonian theory of judicial review. The tendency of the Court to act upon the Hamiltonian theory was carried far under the leadership of Chief Justice Taft and reached a climax under his successor Chief Justice Hughes, though both these eminent jurists were reluctant to go along with a majority of the Court in the most extreme applications of the Hamiltonian doctrine, notably in the judicial veto of federal and state legislation establishing minimum wages for women employed in industry.[23]

In recent years this tendency has happily been reversed. Under the interpretation of the due-process clause, which now tends to prevail, protection of liberty of contract of employers has been abandoned in cases involving measures of the kind envisaged by Justices Harlan and Holmes in their memorable dissenting opinions. At the same time the Court has discovered in the due-process clauses new and more effective defenses against the abridgment of basic human rights. The fundamental freedoms set forth in the first article of the federal Bill of Rights have been brought within the protection of the due-process clauses and made more secure than ever before. The Court has now repudiated the Hamiltonian doctrine and established a Jeffersonian doctrine of judicial review in its stead. In 1931 the freedom of the press was judicially defined and protected against abridgment by the state of Minnesota.[24] In 1937 freedom of speech and of assembly were likewise defined and protected against abridgment by the state of Oregon.[25] In 1940 freedom of religion was protected against abridgment by the state of Connecticut.[26] A long time had passed since Jefferson's avowal of confidence in the "learning and integrity" of judges, but at last his confidence appeared to have been vindicated by the record. Under cover of a new and more reasonable interpretation of the due-process clauses the Supreme Court has at last breathed a Jeffersonian spirit into the text of the Constitution.

The Jeffersonian doctrine of judicial review, like the Hamiltonian, is not always easy to apply. In a score or more of cases, involving the aggressive and often unpopular activities of the religious sect known as Jehovah's Witnesses, the Court has found great difficulty in making up its mind about whose liberty was entitled to protection. The proselyting zeal of this energetic and unmannerly sect caused intense resentment by members of other sects, which was reflected in the adoption of sundry state laws and local ordinances designed to restrict its activities. The Supreme Court decided some points first in one way, then in another, obviously ill at ease in its efforts to find the right adjustment between the rights of an unpopular minority to propagate its faith and those of an offended and hostile majority with greater power to influence legislators and executive officers. The sensational flag-salute cases [27] illustrate the difficulties of judges who are trying to infuse a new spirit of freedom into the fundamental law contrary to the prevailing mood of the public. In the latest case,[28] decided in November 1947, as in several of the earlier cases, the judges were closely divided in opinion. Five of them held that Jehovah's Witnesses should be treated under the Selective Service Act as conscientious objectors, subject to limited service, while four of the judges believed that they should be treated as ministers of the gospel, altogether exempt from service under the act. The liberal spirit, engendered by the cases involving the naturalization of conscientious objectors, had evidently been sorely tried, and without more support from public opinion a majority of the Court seemed no longer disposed to give cantankerous sectarians further benefit of judicial doubt concerning the extent of their constitutional privileges and immunities.

On the whole, the United States Supreme Court has made great advances in recent years in the judicial protection of the constitutional rights of Americans. The adoption of the Jeffersonian, instead of the Hamiltonian, concept of the doctrine of judicial review has for the first time made the federal judges effective guardians of the revolutionary spirit underlying the original declarations and bills of rights. Fundamental freedoms have been secured against abridgment, not only by ill-considered acts of Congress, but also by similar acts of the state governments. Much still remains to be done before the promise of uniform nation-wide judicial protection for basic human rights, held forth by the Fourteenth Amendment, can be deemed to be fulfilled. But the road to the fulfillment of this promise seems at last to be open.

Yet complete protection by judicial action of all that is implied in the American declarations and bills of rights cannot be expected. There are several reasons for this conclusion. Some of them are technical. Judges can act only on the cases that are brought before them and in any case can deal less effectively with acts of omission than with acts of commission. Reluctant co-operation by local authorities makes the task of national officers, judicial or political, excessively difficult. The long struggle to protect the Negro against discrimination in the administration of state election laws and local police regulations offers evidence enough on this point. The debates over the antilynching, antipoll-tax, and fair-employment practices bills in Congress disclose the complexity of this particular part of the general problem. The judges, however unimpeachable may be their learning and integrity, cannot go far ahead of the public opinion by which in the long run they must be sustained.

Moreover, the concept of liberty is not static. It is a dynamic concept, which must be constantly adapted to the changing circumstances under which men live. The necessity of eternal vigilance not only, but also of continual thinking about the nature of basic human rights, was demonstrated by the Hutchins Commission on the Freedom of the Press.[29] This commission set out to answer the question: Is the freedom of the press in danger? Its answer to that question was: Yes! For this answer the commission gave three reasons. The first was that the importance of the press to the people had greatly increased with the development of the press as an instrument of mass communication. At the same time, the commission pointed out, the development of the press as an instrument of mass communication had greatly decreased the proportion of the people who could express their opinions and ideas through the press. Secondly, in the opinion of the commission the few who were able to use the machinery of the press as an instrument of mass communication had not provided a service adequate to the needs of the public. Thirdly, those who directed the machinery of the press seemed to the commission to have engaged in practices which American society condemns and which, if continued, the commission believed, society would inevitably undertake to regulate or control. "When an instrument of prime importance to all the people is available to a small minority of the people only, and when it is employed by that small minority in such a way as not to supply the people with the service they require," the commission concluded, "the freedom of the minority in the employment of that instrument is in danger." Such a situation appears to call for a new concept of freedom of the press or for new efforts on the part of the government to make the existing freedom more widely serviceable. Such a task is not for judges, but for public opinion, and for the agencies of the people directly responsible to the public.

Finally, the federal judges are bound to observe the constitutional distinction between the privileges and immunities of Americans and those of the people of the several states. The state judges are still primarily responsible for the protection of the rights of New Yorkers, Virginians, Mississippians, and Californians. Experience shows that the state judges will reflect the strong and preponderant opinion among the people of their respective states rather than the best thinking of the whole body of people. So far as the basic human rights of Americans are threatened by the discriminatory behavior of private citizens, the victims of discrimination must still for the most part look to the state lawmakers and the state judges for protection. Experience shows, also, that these victims cannot expect to enjoy equal protection in all the states in the existing state of opinion among the people of the several states.

The recent report of the President's Committee on Civil
Rights [30] has made this fact abundantly clear. It contains
thirty-five specific recommendations for increasing the
security of the fundamental freedoms of one class of Americans, namely, the Negroes. These recommendations are
designed to strengthen the machinery for the protection of
civil rights, to strengthen the right to safety and security of
the person, to strengthen the right to citizenship and its
privileges, to strengthen the right to freedom of conscience
and expression, to strengthen the right to equality of opportunity, and to rally the American people to the support of
a continuing program to strengthen civil rights. This last
recommendation called for a long-term campaign of public
education to inform the people of the civil rights to which
they are entitled and of the duties which they owe one
another. The public-opinion polls have disclosed the urgency
of such a campaign. The need for a popular civil-rights
campaign in America more than a century and a half after
the adoption of the revolutionary declarations and bills of
rights is a sobering fact which may well be borne in mind
by those who are planning an international bill of rights
for the nations of the world.

The Privileges and Immunities of Citizens of the United Nations

THE experience of the people of the United States in promoting respect for human rights suggests that there is a wide difference between the rights of the peoples of particular nations in their own countries and the privileges and immunities of members of the whole body of peoples comprising the United Nations. The claim of the American people to inalienable rights was staked out in the Declaration of Independence, but the Supreme Court has been very slow to read such rights into the privileges and immunities of citizens of the United States. A few basic principles of government have been read into the body of the Constitution, and a considerable quantity of advice, not always good, concerning legislative policies has been read into the due-process clauses of the Fifth and Fourteenth Amendments. Until recently the guardians of the fundamental freedoms of Americans were primarily the lawmakers and judges of the several states. The state bills of rights, sustained by the organized opinion of the people of the states, were in principle until 1868, and, in fact, until long afterward, the principal security for basic human rights in the United States. In the light of American experience must we not expect that the fundamental freedoms of mankind under the Charter of the United Nations will depend mainly upon the different attitudes of the various peoples within the member states?

The experience of the American people suggests also an awkward ambiguity in the idea of basic human rights. Assuming that the people of the several states possess such

The Notes to this lecture begin on page 154.

rights, there is still the problem of determining what they are. Presumably both New Yorkers and Virginians, for example, possess the same fundamental human rights, but, in fact, their patterns of behavior in the ordinary relationships of man to man are far from identical. Virginians, for instance, maintain the policy of segregation as a proper rule for governing the relationship between the white and black races. New Yorkers strive to diminish the importance of racial distinctions both in the laws and in the customs of their state. Fundamental human rights may be regarded as those rights only which the two people have in common and respect and observe alike. This view of the nature of such rights may be described as realistic. It reduces the essential rights of Virginians and New Yorkers under the existing circumstances to something less than the whole body of liberties actually enjoyed by the people of either state. A realistic view diminishes the danger of conflict between the two people concerning their fundamental human rights. It also diminishes the importance of the concept of such rights. It is indeed realistic, but it is uninspiring.

The other view of the nature of basic human rights regards them as a body of political, economic, and social ideals. This is the view which Lincoln maintained as the proper explanation of the American proposition that all men are created equal. In accordance with this view, the different opinions which tend to prevail in New York and Virginia concerning the segregation of the white and black races need not result in excluding both of them from the concept of basic human rights. An adequate declaration of rights should include either the right of white and black men to live segregated lives or the right of members of the two races to equal and uniform treatment in all human relationships without any distinction on account of color. The idealistic view requires a choice between conflicting opinions concerning the desirable relations between the white and black races, and the acceptance of one of the conflicting patterns of interracial behavior and the rejection of the other by both peoples. This view means that the concept of basic human rights will apply to those areas of conduct in which different patterns of behavior are competing for public acceptance. It means that people who believe strongly that their own behavior patterns are right will strive by every means to enforce their principles of right upon those who disagree with them. The idealistic view is dynamic and stimulating; it is also provocative and disturbing.

The normal consequences of this way of looking at the basic human rights are strikingly illustrated at the present time by the prolonged and bitter controversy in Congress over the antilynching, antipoll-tax, and fair-employment practices bills. The constitutional agencies of the Federal Government have not been able to settle these controversies over human rights promptly. Some have remained unsettled for a long time. But the method of political and judicial settlement is so far superior to war that people can tolerate some injustices as long as they can hope for a rational settlement without too much delay. The agencies for the political settlement of disputes over basic human rights between the peoples of different states under the Constitution of the United States, however, are greatly superior to those provided by the Charter of the United Nations for the settlement of disputes concerning basic human rights among the peoples of the United Nations. The relations among members of the United Nations under the Charter are very different from those among the states of the American Union under the Constitution. A better analogy would be that among members of the United Nations and among states of the American Union under the Articles of Confederation before the adoption of the Constitution.

The government of the United Nations is comparable in many interesting ways to that of the United States under the Articles of Confederation. It does not deal directly with the peoples of the member nations, but depends on the collaboration and support of their several governments. It has no power to tax these peoples, or to regulate com-

75

merce among them, or to enforce its recommendations and decisions except by its moral influence over their several governments, or, in the last extremity, by waging war against them. The Charter of the United Nations is in one important respect a more promising foundation for an effective system of government than the Articles of Confederation. It can be amended by something less than the unanimous consent of its members. To be sure, any one of the permanent members of the Security Council can block the adoption of amendments to the Charter. But the Charter in its present form does provide a promising procedure for the preparation and adoption of conventions for dealing with particular situations, such as the promotion of respect for fundamental freedoms, designed to be effective between those member nations that become parties to them.

The Charter of the United Nations, like the Articles of Confederation, fails to determine specifically who shall be citizens. It does not even contain any provisions like those in Article 4 of the Articles of Confederation, which secured to the free inhabitants of each of the states all the privileges and immunities of free citizens in the several states. This article also provided that the people of each state should have free ingress and regress to and from any other state, and should enjoy therein all the privileges of trade and commerce, subject to the same conditions generally as the inhabitants thereof. Nor is there any provision in the United Nations Charter for giving full faith and credit in each of the nations to official proceedings in the other member nations. The Charter is written in the names of the peoples of the United Nations. It contains no reference to a single body of people of the United Nations as a whole. It is too soon to say that the people of the United Nations constitute one nation. It may be that the peoples of the member states will eventually be recognized as citizens of the United Nations, and as members of a single community entitled to pass and repass through every part of it without interruption, as freely as in their respective states. But to achieve such a freedom is not among the declared purposes of the United Nations. The purpose that is declared with reference to human rights is not to establish the privileges and immunities of a single body of United Nations citizens by direct action on the part of the United Nations Organization. It is to achieve international co-operation in promoting and encouraging respect for human rights, that is to say, to bring about action by the member states, presumably each acting on its own authority within its own jurisdiction.

The great difficulty that stands in the way of achieving this purpose is the loyalty of the peoples of the United Nations to the purposes and principles of their own particular states. These purposes and principles are set forth in the declarations and bills of rights of these states. Whatever may be the legalistic doctrine concerning the sovereignty of the members of the United Nations, the stubborn fact is that their peoples naturally place greater confidence in the institutions with which they are familiar than in any international organization, which is still new and largely untried. If such an organization proposes an international bill of rights containing novel doctrines and strange procedures, its proposals are likely to be regarded with suspicion. The peoples of the United Nations at this stage in the development of a general international organization naturally regard their own customary or recently acquired liberties and their own political ideals with greater favor than those which are alien and perhaps apparently hostile to their own.

How formidable this difficulty may be becomes clear when the content of the American declarations and bills of rights is compared with that of the corresponding documents of the other leading members of the United Nations. Consider, for example, the various different national attitudes toward the group of rights suggested by the expressions, a right to work or a right to full employment. In fact, neither the federal Bill of Rights nor any of the state declarations and bills mentions such a right. The opposition of the American Bar Association to the approval of a so-called right to work

77

helped to prevent the adoption of the report of its Committee on Human Rights. The opposition of congressmen to a right to full employment resulted in the exclusion of that phrase from the Employment Act of 1946.

How different is the situation in the Soviet Union! Chapter X of the Stalin constitution begins with an article relating to the right to work. "Citizens of the Soviet Union," this article, which is actually number 118 in the constitution, declares, "have the right to guaranteed employment and payment for their work in accordance with its quantity and quality." This seems to fall far short of the original Communist slogan, "from each according to his ability, to each according to his needs." In order to make more clear the nature of this right to work Article 118 provides further, "It is insured by the Socialist organization of the national economy, the steady growth of the productive forces of Soviet society, the absence of economic crises, and the abolition of unemployment." The right to work, as thus defined, seems to be the expression of a hope of reaching eventually a distant goal, or at most a declaration of legislative policy. It is supplemented in the two following articles by the right to rest and leisure and the right of maintenance in old age and also in case of sickness or loss of capacity to work. These three articles together outline a program of social security, which is offered to the Soviet citizen in lieu of the pure Communist principle of remuneration according to need regardless of the individual's actual contribution to production. This substitute for the essential principle of genuine Communism is evidently deemed more immediately practicable in this transitory period, in which the state has not yet withered away and much remains to be done before the ultimate goals of the Marxist revolution will be within reach. In short, this fundamental freedom of contemporary Russians is a compromise between the traditional aspirations of revolutionary Marxists and the practical notions of Communist bureaucrats charged with responsibility for the production of goods in the Soviet Union.

The Privileges and Immunities of Citizens

The provisions of the constitution of the Fourth French Republic, like those of the Stalin constitution, reflect the consequences of political compromise for the purpose of reaching an acceptable adjustment between the aspirations of the individual and the obligations of the state. Among the principles proclaimed in the preamble to the French constitution, as finally adopted, one of the first is that everyone has the duty to work and the right to obtain employment. The preamble further provides that no one may suffer in his work on account of his origins, opinions, or beliefs. This suggests that a Frenchman has great freedom to criticize his employer and even to profess a belief in unpopular creeds such as Communism. Moreover, the right of the worker to participate in trade-union action and to join the union of his choice is expressly noted in the preamble as well as the right to strike. The latter right, however, must be exercised "within the framework of the laws that govern it," whatever that may mean. The preamble also contains guarantees of rest and leisure as well as protection against the hazards of age, sickness, and involuntary unemployment.

The framers of the French constitution were trying to draft a document that would be acceptable to the members of the three principal parties in contemporary French politics, the Communists, the Socialists, and the Popular Republicans. This involved putting something into the constitution desired by each party, or striking a mean of some sort between the views of all. The former policy was difficult as the framers of the first draft constitution had already discovered, since including in a declaration of rights provisions satisfactory to Communists would antagonize Popular Republicans and the principles satisfactory to Popular Republicans would antagonize Communists. The mean between them, at least in what concerned provisions suitable to a new economic bill of rights, was substantially the ground occupied by the Socialists, and this part of the original draft constitution was essentially a Socialist document. The corresponding provisions in the draft that was finally adopted were also essentially socialistic, but designed to be less offensive both to the Communists on the left and the Popular Republicans on the right. The conflicting attitudes which had to be reconciled in the constitution varied more widely than any that needed to be considered by the authors of the Stalin constitution in the Soviet Union, but the result in the one case as in the other was manifestly a compromise. The form of the compromise was different, since the conditions of the people of the two countries and the circumstances under which the compromises were made were different. Evidently also agreement between members of the French and Russian nations upon principles relating to the right to work will also be difficult as long as the governments of the Fourth French Republic and of the Soviet Union continue to be what they are.

In England there is no formal declaration of a right to work. The Labour party, which is in power, is committed to some policies designed to strengthen the position of the workers and to improve the conditions of employment. The Conservative party presumably maintains a hostile attitude toward these policies. Perhaps as fair a statement as any of the attitude of Englishmen, belonging to the governing party, concerning the right to work is that found in Sir William Beveridge's *Full Employment in a Free Society*.[1] This significant book was published by a leading theorist of the British labor movement on the eve of its conquest of power at the general election of 1945. In this book Beveridge attempts to describe the essentials of what he regards as a free society. Beveridge does not mention a right to work in so many words, but he does specify among the essentials of a free society freedom in the choice of an occupation and freedom in the management of personal income. The list of essential liberties which he compiles in this connection, however, does not include the liberty of a private citizen to own the means of production or to employ other citizens in operating them at a wage. That is to say, Beveridge does not include a freedom of business enterprise among the essentials of a free society.

The American bills of rights contain no mention of any freedom of business enterprise. Such a freedom, however, was read into the language of the federal Bill of Rights by the Supreme Court in a long series of decisions which reached a climax under the leadership of Chief Justice Taft.[2] Though this basic freedom has been subjected to some important limitations in recent years, the New Deal Court's concept of freedom of contract and other elements of economic freedom preserves more of the free-enterprise system than would be acceptable to the British Labour party, to say nothing of French Socialists and Russian Communists.[3] Evidently agreement by these peoples upon the contents of anything that could be described as an economic bill of rights would be so exceedingly difficult as to render the attempt to reach it unattractive to practical politicians in any of these countries. Agreement might be reached by the adoption of language so vague and ambiguous as to admit various interpretations, suited to the prevailing attitudes among the different nations, but the value of a fundamental freedom so variously understood in promoting better working conditions in the different countries of the world would be dubious. In this country, for instance, we have professed belief in the fundamental nature of freedom from want, and we also have the Taft-Hartley Act. The provisions of the Taft-Hartley Act cannot be altogether reconciled with the economic liberties set forth in the preamble of the constitution of the Fourth French Republic or professed by the British Labour party. Yet Americans in their present mood would not agree to a provision in an international bill of rights that would outlaw the economic policy contained in that piece of legislation.

Next to the right to work in the Stalin constitution is the right to education. This right, according to Article 121, is ensured by universal compulsory elementary education, by the fact that "education, including higher education, is free of charge by the system of state scholarships for the over-whelming majority of students in the higher schools, by instruction in schools being conducted in the native language (that is, the language of the scholars whatever it may be) and the organization of free vocational technical and agro-nomic training for the toilers in the factories, state farms, machine and tractor stations, and collective farms." Much of this article on education has a modern sound to the peoples of the West, but it says nothing about one of the most controversial aspects of freedom of education in the West. Does educational freedom mean that anybody can organize a school and offer instruction of whatever kind he pleases to those who may be persuaded to attend? Or does educational freedom mean that education is free to all in schools organized by the government and conducted in accordance with the official views concerning sound educa-tional policy? May the public schools monopolize the time for study of all the children, or may religious bodies, for instance, or atheists organize schools of their own and insist that time be allowed for attendance at such schools by those who wish to do so? May they even demand grants of public money to enable such schools to maintain the standards of service established for the public schools?

The answer of the Russian constitution to these questions is simple and direct. Article 124 provides that "in order to ensure to citizens freedom of conscience, the church in the U.S.S.R. is separated from the State, and the school from the church. Freedom of religious worship," it adds, "and freedom of anti-religious propaganda are recognized for all citizens." These provisions ensure an educational mo-nopoly to the public schools. How much freedom of religious propaganda is secured along with freedom of religious worship is not clear, but there is nothing to suggest any freedom for religious education apart from religious wor-ship. Even this limited recognition of religious freedom represents a compromise between the earlier proscription of public religious worship and the broad interpretation of religious liberty which has been encouraged by the Supreme Court of the United States in the cases brought before the Court in recent years by the sect of Jehovah's Witnesses.[4]

The framers of the constitution of the Fourth French Republic found one of the most difficult problems with which they had to deal to be the desire of many Frenchmen to include in the freedom of education not only a right for the Roman Catholic church to maintain professional schools for training priests and ministers of religion, but also a right to propagate the faith through a system of popular elementary schools. This might mean either to give religious instruction to ordinary scholars along with instruction of other kinds in special church schools or to give religious instruction to children belonging to the church but attending the public schools. There was the further question of who should pay for such instruction, if it should be allowed. This controversy the framers of the French constitution found beyond their capacity to settle, and the preamble, as finally adopted, provides merely that the nation guarantees equal access of the child and the adult to instruction, to vocational training, and to culture. It adds that the organization of free and secular public education at all stages is a duty of the state, but it omits all reference to any right of Frenchmen to organize church schools for the special benefit of children belonging to a particular religious sect. The right of members of religious sects to give instruction in state schools seems to be denied. Such an adjustment of the conflicting interests of the advocates and opponents of a comprehensive and secular public-school system may be well suited to the needs of contemporary French politics. It can hardly be regarded as a final statement of a basic human right to an education.

Englishmen can find nothing about a right to education in any official list of fundamental freedoms. The existence of an established church in England encouraged a greater reliance on church schools than in France and impeded the establishment of a nonsectarian system of free public schools.

The development of a comprehensive school system under public control has proceeded rapidly in recent years, but there is no such conflict between the church schools and those of the state as has raged in France. The policy of the government has been more tolerant both of church and other private schools and of religious instruction in state schools than in France. In view of the diverse educational and religious traditions of the two countries there would be difficulty in agreeing upon a uniform statement of fundamental freedoms in the field of education. Freedom of worship is a concept that would certainly carry different implications in the two countries. If the framers of the constitution for the Fourth French Republic were unable to agree upon an acceptable formula for the regulation of the relations between church, school, and state, how much more troublesome would be the task of finding a common formula upon which both Englishmen and Frenchmen could stand together!

In the United States there is nothing definite about a right to education in the federal Bill of Rights, but the state constitutions are full of provisions designed to encourage the development of systems of popular education under public control in which instruction shall be free and nonsectarian. The principle of the separation of church and state was established by the first article of the federal Bill of Rights, though such a separation was not generally the practice in the original states. Many states now expressly forbid the appropriation of public money for schools not under public control, and some expressly forbid religious instruction of any kind in the public schools. At the same time there has been general toleration of religious and other private schools, and sporadic attempts to establish educational monopolies for the public schools or to interfere unduly with instruction in church and private schools have been discouraged by the Supreme Court.[5] Church and other private schools flourish alongside the public schools, and the adjustment of the relations between them remains to be determined upon any uniform principle.

The Privileges and Immunities of Citizens

Recent cases have raised for the first time fundamental questions concerning the meaning of the separation of church and state under the federal Constitution.[6] One of these involved the right of the state of New Jersey to authorize the appropriation of public money to defray the cost of transporting children to parochial schools as well as to public schools. The Supreme Court held that the First Amendment had erected a wall between church and state. "That wall," declared Justice Black, speaking for a majority of the Court, "must be kept high and impregnable. We could not approve the slightest breach." But when he added that New Jersey had not breached it in that case, four of the judges dissented. The dissenting judges made clear their devotion to the traditional American principle of separation of church and state, but failed to clarify the application of the principle to the problem of state grants-in-aid toward the support of education in schools not under public control. The latest case resulted in a decision ending an arrangement in Champaign, Illinois, for religious education in the public schools by representatives of leading churches. One judge dissented, and the majority required three separate opinions to state their views satisfactorily. Apparently there would be as much difficulty in the United States as in France in agreeing upon a systematic and comprehensive statement, covering all the implications of a right to education, including therein a right to establish private schools, to receive grants of public money for defraying in part at least the costs of instruction therein, and to enjoy some degree of immunity against public control.

The difficulty of reaching an agreement among the major powers upon the content of educational freedom is enhanced by the varieties of opinion concerning who shall teach and what shall be taught. In the Soviet Union the right to education does not explicitly include a right to teach. While there is nothing in the constitution restricting that right expressly to Communists, the spirit of the constitution is clearly hostile to any claim by non-Communists of a right to teach in the public schools. In the United States recent proposals to apply the same policy in reverse, that is, to exclude Communist teachers from the public schools, and to deny them the right to establish private schools at their own expense, have provoked spirited differences of opinion. Presumably the Supreme Court would not sustain a state law, discriminating against Communists in the exercise of whatever right to teach may be included in their general right to freedom of speech, as long as they do not incite their pupils to violence or create a clear and present danger of a forcible overthrow of the government. Be that as it may, it does not seem likely that under the present conditions there could be an international agreement upon a right to education except in the most general terms. Such willful obfuscation as would be necessary to secure universal consent to inclusion of a comprehensive right to education in an international bill of rights would be more likely to impair than to promote respect for fundamental freedoms among the leading peoples of the modern world.

Any searching discussion of a right to education leads eventually to consideration of the fundamental freedoms of speech and of the press. The constitutions of all the major powers contain provisions dealing with these basic human rights. The Soviet constitution of 1936 does not put these rights at the head of the list, but neither does it ignore them. Article 125 provides "that in conformity with the interests of the toilers and in order to strengthen the socialist system, the citizens of the U.S.S.R. are guaranteed: freedom of speech; freedom of the press; freedom of assembly and of holding mass meetings; and freedom of street processions and demonstrations." This article goes on to specify the means for securing these fundamental freedoms to citizens of the Soviet Union. "These rights of the citizens," it states, "are ensured by placing at the disposal of the toilers and their organizations printing presses, supplies of paper, public buildings, the streets, means of communication and other material requisites for the exercise of these rights." The understanding of these basic human rights in the Soviet Union is manifestly different from that in the United States. In the Soviet Union emphasis is laid upon practical access to facilities and materials essential for communicating ideas to fellow citizens, but these facilities are restricted to "toilers" and presumably are not available to those who do not "toil." It will not be easy to reconcile such a concept of freedom with ideas long and firmly cherished in the United States.

The next article in the constitution of the Soviet Union deals with the right of association, an essential concomitant of the basic rights of free speech and a free press. "In conformity with the interests of the toilers," it states, "and in order to develop the organizational initiative and political activity of the masses of the people, citizens of the U.S.S.R. are insured the right to unite in public organizations,—trade unions, cooperative associations, youth organizations, sport and defense organizations, cultural, technical, and scientific societies; and the most active and politically conscious citizens from among the working class and other strata of the toilers unite in the Communist Party of the U.S.S.R., which is the vanguard of the toilers in their struggle to strengthen and develop the socialist system and which represents the leading core of all organizations of the toilers, both social and state." The right of organization is evidently regarded as of equal importance with the other fundamental freedoms of speech and of the press, but the right to organize a political party is treated as the special prerogative of a privileged class; namely, those citizens deemed to be the most active and politically conscious among the toilers. The grant of such a high privilege to a special class makes a breach in the system of equal rights that must seem utterly alien and irrational to peoples sharing in the American, English, or French heritage of political ideas.

This peculiar Soviet attitude explains what would otherwise appear unintelligible in the attitude toward basic human rights, as understood in the West, by spokesmen of the

Soviet Union in the General Assembly of the United Nations.[7] Mr. Vyshinsky, for instance, in his address to the General Assembly, September 19, 1947, referred to what he called "a furious campaign in the press, mainly in the American press and in the press of the countries following the United States obediently, like Turkey. This campaign," he declared, "has been spread already for a considerable period of time for the purpose of coaxing public opinion in favor of a new war." Such a press campaign he professed to regard as unrepresentative of the true feelings of the American people. "All this press," he added, "is entirely in the hands of the bosses of various newspaper enterprises, and does what it is ordered, claiming their literature to be the expression of public opinion." Nevertheless, in most cases, he asserted, it would be impossible for the people to speak of their needs and wishes in books, magazines, and newspapers published in millions of copies. Thus, he concluded, the opinions of the owners of the newspapers could masquerade as public opinion.

This Russian concept of freedom of mass communications called for action by the United Nations against propaganda for a new war. In pursuance of this thought the delegations of the Soviet Union at the General Assembly submitted a set of resolutions, one of which declared that the tolerance of such propaganda was a violation of the obligations undertaken by the members of the United Nations. Another declared that their governments should prohibit such propaganda in any form and should take measures for its effective prevention and suppression. These resolutions became the basis of a bitter campaign against the so-called crime of warmongering. Should such a crime be recognized by law in the United States? Should the government not only provide for the punishment of warmongers, but also exercise such control over the press as may be necessary to prevent the commission of the crime? In short, must the Government of the United States establish a censorship of the press in order to satisfy a basic requirement of an international bill of rights?

It is evident from even a hasty inspection of the constitutions of the major powers in the modern world that their respective peoples already possess characteristic but by no means uniform versions of three of President Roosevelt's Four Freedoms. It should be easy for the major powers to agree to respect a freedom of speech and of expression, if each is to be free also to put its own interpretation upon this freedom. It should be easy likewise to agree to respect the freedom of worship, and the freedom from want, upon the same condition. Inspection of the constitutions of the major powers does not enable any statement to be made with the same confidence concerning the freedom from fear. But if the logical implications of the other three fundamental freedoms are to be meticulously spelled out in an international bill of rights, it is by no means clear that the major powers can co-operate in promoting universal respect for, and observance of, such freedoms.

On the contrary, inspection of the provisions of the latest constitutions and laws, relating to the fundamental freedoms, discloses plainly the formidable difficulties that stand in the way of general agreement upon an international bill of rights dealing boldly and explicitly with the important issues of our time. The prevalent conceptions of basic human rights are preconditioned by the nature of the various economic and social orders which exist among the leading peoples of the world. We Americans, for instance, find explicit constitutional discrimination against the members of any particular economic or social class repugnant to our ideas of ordered freedom. Discrimination against property owners, as a class, is particularly repugnant to Americans who have been devoted to the principle, as they understand it, of equal rights for all classes alike. In Great Britain, however, still more in France, and above all in the Soviet Union, discrimination against certain classes seems less objectionable than discrimination on account of race, language, or religion. Evidently, if an international bill of rights is to be comprehensive and specific, agreement upon its contents among nations so different in their attitudes toward current political controversies as the peoples of the Soviet Union, the Fourth French Republic, the United Kingdom, and the United States can be accomplished only by the acceptance of ingenious compromises, which are likely to be generally unsatisfactory, if not meaningless. The alternatives are either a comprehensive and specific bill of rights, which will not be acceptable to all the major powers of the modern world, or a bill of rights, which, like the American Declaration of Independence, will not attempt to do more than declare some general objectives of political action.

The International Declaration on Human Rights, proposed by the United Nations Commission on Human Rights, is a normal product of the times. It meets the traditional requirements of a declaration of rights by dealing with most of the topics covered in the classic declarations of the eighteenth century. It deals also with the principal topics deemed essential for a modern economic bill of rights. It attempts to establish standards for guidance in the practical realization of the new ideal of a freedom from want as well as of the old ideals of civil and religious liberty. But it does not attempt to deal directly and specifically with the ideal of a freedom from fear. Fear of aggression may be dispelled, its authors presumably believe, by the improvement of international relations which would follow the growth of respect for and observance of other fundamental freedoms among the peoples of the world. Its hopes for such a growth of better international feeling are plainly bound up with the success of its proposal for a separate covenant designed to incorporate its list of fundamental freedoms in the law of nations. But the Commission does not propose any improvements in the organization of the United Nations to give greater security to a new freedom from fear.

The content of the proposed International Declaration on Human Rights follows the model of the revolutionary declarations more closely than that of the revolutionary bills. It contains a number of articles setting forth general principles of government based upon the political experience of the West. It contains also a considerable amount of good advice relating not only to the traditional topics but also to those with which modern governments are more particularly concerned. For example, the family deriving from marriage, we are told, is the natural and fundamental group unit of society. Men and women, the text of the draft continues, shall have the same freedom to contract marriage in accordance with law. Marriage and the family, this portion of the text concludes, shall be protected by the state and society. There are also a number of articles that propose substantive and procedural limitations upon the authority and the processes of national governments. Some of these general principles of government and much of this advice are obviously well-intentioned, if not very explicit. They should receive widespread, if not universal, approval. The effect of the articles which proclaim the desirability of limitations upon the power of national governments will, of course, depend mainly upon the fate of the corresponding provisions in the proposed Covenant.

Judgment upon the principles of government and the good advice contained in the proposed International Declaration must be based largely upon the treatment of the controversial topics. If these topics are treated ambiguously, or evaded altogether, the practical utility of the Declaration under the strenuous conditions of the modern world is likely to be small. If, on the other hand, they are faced boldly, and a vigorous effort is made to formulate ideals, capable of appealing powerfully to some, at least, of the peoples of the world, the Declaration may profoundly influence the course of events. The nature of its influence would depend upon whose ideals were preferred by the framers of the Declaration. Its extent would depend upon how vigorous were the efforts to make the preferred ideals prevail in the ensuing conflict.

The most controversial issues are those which grow out of the effort to deal with the freedom from want. They concern the right to work and the right to own private property. The article of the proposed Declaration, relating to the latter right, provides that "everyone has the right to own property in conformity with the laws of the state in which such property is located. No one," it adds, "shall be arbitrarily deprived of his property." The first part of this article evades the main issue by making the right contingent upon the policy of the state having jurisdiction over the property. It sanctions a capitalistic system of private property in the United States, a socialistic system in Great Britain and France, and a communistic system in the Soviet Union. The second part of the article throws the emphasis on the legal procedures which give vitality to the word "arbitrarily." The practical significance of such a provision depends upon the actual processes of government which may be promoted by the relevant provisions of the proposed Covenant.

The treatment of the right to work in the proposed Declaration is equally evasive. "Everyone," the article on the subject begins, "has the right to work." This statement obviously requires further elucidation. The article continues: "The state has a duty to take such measures as may be within its powers to ensure that all persons ordinarily resident within its territory have an opportunity for useful work." Upon reading this sentence it is hard to know which to admire more, the ingenuity of the framers of this article in finding a formula to which persons of the most contrary opinions could subscribe, or their prudence in declining to commit themselves to a choice between the sides of an irrepressible ideological conflict. The framers apparently realized that something more on this topic was required of them. The article concludes: "The state is bound to take all necessary steps to prevent unemployment." The expression "full employment," so detestable to many Americans, is artfully avoided, but to what country shall the inhabitants of backward regions, seeking light and inspiration from such a declaration, look for guidance in the development of a policy concerning labor-management relations, to the United States or to the Soviet Union?

The right to education is treated with greater elaboration but with equal circumspection. "Everyone," the pertinent article begins, "has the right to education. Fundamental education shall be free and compulsory. There shall be equal access for higher education as can be provided by the state or community on the basis of merit and without distinction as to race, sex, language, religion, social standing, financial means or political affiliation." The framers believed in education and made clear their desire that it should be rightly directed. "Education will be directed," they accordingly added, "to the full intellectual, physical, moral and spiritual development of the human personality, to the strengthening of respect for human rights and fundamental freedoms, and to the combating of the spirit of intolerance and hatred against other nations or racial or religious groups anywhere." This is excellent advice, but what light does it throw on the right of religious bodies to establish private-school systems and to demand financial support for such schools from the public treasury? The framers of the Declaration wished to make some provision for the protection of ethnic, linguistic, and religious minorities that might desire to establish separate schools of their own, but were unable to agree upon a suitable text. Two different texts were proposed, but neither of these ventures to deal with the vexatious question of state subsidies for such schools.

The Commission on Human Rights did not try to deal with the fundamental issues involved in any effective security for the freedom of speech and of the press and of participation in the use of modern systems of communicating intelligence. The whole subject was referred for consideration to the International Conference on Freedom of Information at Geneva. It is clear enough to Americans that the difficulties to be overcome in dealing with this subject effectively are great. Our own treatment of the use of the radio is unsatisfactory, but we do not wish to entrust the government with a radio monopoly as in many foreign countries. We may not like warmongering, but neither do we like governmental censorship. No problem could illustrate more clearly the difference between a fundamental human right and a sound policy for a particular country in a particular stage of the development of its communication services. We do not wish to subscribe to an international declaration that would seriously restrict our freedom to experiment with various policies for the regulation of the broadcasting industry, or for the discouragement of incitement to violence and war. Should we join in an attempt to prescribe policies regarding such problems to the peoples of other countries?

An appraisal of the recent report of the Commission on Human Rights cannot disregard the unsatisfactory treatment of these controversial topics. There seems little to be gained by the adoption of detailed and ambiguous statements, which purport to deal with specific problems of contemporary politics, but which can neither settle the ideological conflicts between major powers nor give intelligible guidance to the peoples of backward regions. What is the advantage of such a detailed but uninspiring declaration over the simple enunciation of inalienable rights in the American Declaration of Independence? That declaration, it is true, was highly generalized and even ambiguous. It has been the basis of much controversy in the course of the years. But it has served well its essential purpose. It has defined a goal of rational endeavor which successive generations have interpreted according to the varying needs of their time. The use that Lincoln made of its timeless statement of American political ideals stands as a monument to the wisdom of true statesmanship. For the primary educational purposes of a declaration of rights it is hard to improve upon the immortal work of Jefferson.

Final judgment upon the work of the Commission on Human Rights must be withheld pending examination of its proposed Covenant. The provisions for enriching the law of nations and for limiting the authority and improving the processes of the governments of the members of the United Nations do not depend solely, or perhaps even mainly, upon the fortunes of the proposed Declaration. But the Declaration cannot be passed over without noting that its framers have said nothing about the privileges and immunities of citizens of the United Nations, regarded as members of a single body of people. The Commission on Human Rights seems to assume that the United Nations are as far advanced in their collective political development as the United States after the adoption of the Fourteenth Amendment. Yet its proposals do not treat the privileges and immunities of citizens of the United Nations even as constructively as the privileges and immunities of American citizens were treated under the imperfect Articles of Confederation before the adoption of the Constitution of 1787. American experience, to be sure, does not justify a confident expectation that it will be easy to secure those rights of citizens of the United Nations, which should be distinguished from their rights as citizens of particular member states. But it does suggest strongly that this is the task that should be undertaken first by a general international organization such as the United Nations.

The Problem of Enforcement

THE provisions of the Charter of the United Nations that relate to the problem of enforcing respect for human rights are less definite than those relating to the purpose of promoting such respect. Article 2, which sets forth the principles in accordance with which the United Nations shall act in pursuit of its purposes, imposes upon all members an explicit duty to fulfill in good faith the obligations assumed by them under the Charter. This would seem to imply a duty to respect and observe whatever freedoms the United Nations shall find to be fundamental. Unfortunately, the organization is based expressly on the principle of the sovereign equality of all its members. Although the structure and functions of the Security Council and the privileges of its permanent members cast doubt on the sanctity of this principle, its presence among the declared principles of the United Nations puts a cloud on the title of the organization to the fulfillment by its members of duties which run counter to the principles on which their own governments may be formed.

This implied limitation upon the power of the United Nations to achieve international co-operation in promoting respect for human rights and fundamental freedoms is supported by another important provision of Article 2. Section 7 states explicitly that nothing contained in the Charter shall authorize the United Nations to intervene in matters which are essentially within the domestic jurisdiction of any state or shall require members to submit such matters to settlement under the Charter. This limitation, it is added, shall not prejudice action of the Security Council with respect to "threats to the peace, breaches of the peace, and acts of

---

The Notes to this lecture begin on page 155.

aggression." Subject to this exception, however, it is the clear intention of the framers of the Charter to prevent interference by the United Nations in the domestic affairs of the members. This limitation might seem to make the United Nations incapable of effective action for the purpose of promoting universal respect for, and observance of, human rights and fundamental freedoms.

The effect of this general limitation upon the authority of the United Nations must be estimated in the light of certain other important provisions of the Charter. In the first place, there is Article 14 in the chapter dealing with the functions and powers of the General Assembly. This body, it is provided in Article 14, may "recommend measures for the peaceful adjustment of any situation, regardless of origin, which it deems likely to impair the general welfare or friendly relations among nations." This article specifically includes under the competence of the General Assembly the power to make such recommendations in situations resulting from a violation of the provisions of the Charter setting forth the purposes and principles of the United Nations. It follows, therefore, that, if a disturbing situation should develop resulting from the nonobservance of obligations established by an international bill of rights, the General Assembly may make recommendations for the purpose of improving friendly relations among the nations which have been disturbed by such nonobservance, notwithstanding the prohibition against intervention in the domestic affairs of the member nations. To what extent the provisions of this article enable the United Nations to enforce respect for human rights and fundamental freedoms, even if such action involves some interference in domestic matters, only experience can determine. But it would seem that the General Assembly might go far for the purpose of giving effect to its obligation to achieve international co-operation in promoting such respect, if supported by a strong and preponderant opinion among the delegations of the member nations in the General Assembly.

Further light is thrown upon this problem by some of the provisions of Chapter VI, dealing with the pacific settlement of disputes by the Security Council, and of Chapter VII, authorizing action with respect to threats to the peace, breaches of the peace, and acts of aggression. Article 34 of Chapter VI authorizes the Security Council to determine whether the continuance of a dispute or situation is likely to endanger peace or security. Such a dispute or situation might easily grow out of neglect or willful refusal by a member nation to pay proper respect to the basic human rights of persons subject to its jurisdiction. Such neglect or willful refusal might jeopardize the rights of a minority of its population, if a misguided majority were to adopt measures oppressive to minorities of their fellow citizens, as happened in certain Central European countries in the years preceding World War II. It might even happen that an arbitrary and dictatorial government would oppress all its subjects. In this case the form of government itself might constitute a situation leading to international friction and giving rise to a dispute, the continuance of which would endanger the maintenance of international peace. Such a situation would undoubtedly present a problem of great difficulty to the Security Council. That circumstance, however, would not deprive it of the authority under the Charter to intervene, notwithstanding that the situation was originally a matter essentially within the jurisdiction of the particular state directly concerned.

The investigatory power of the Security Council under Article 34 is confirmed and strengthened by the provisions of Article 39, relating to action with respect to threats to the peace, breaches of the peace, and acts of aggression. Under this article it is the duty of the Council to determine the existence of any threat to the peace and to make recommendations for maintaining and securing international peace. If the Security Council finds, therefore, that the basic human rights and fundamental freedoms of some persons have been abridged by the government of the country in which they reside so as to threaten a disturbance of the general peace, it is bound to decide what measures should be taken in order to ensure the fulfillment in good faith of obligations assumed by members of the United Nations under the Charter. Whether or not this violation is regarded by the government of that member nation as a matter essentially within its domestic jurisdiction, doubtless the practical application of this principle would raise questions of extreme difficulty, which would test the authority and resourcefulness of the Security Council to the utmost, particularly if the offending state were a major power. Whatever may be the practical difficulties which stand in the way of effective enforcement in such cases, it seems to be a reasonable inference from the language of the Charter that the immunity of member states against interference in their domestic affairs does not authorize them to disregard with impunity their obligation to respect the basic human rights of their subjects.

Another important provision of the Charter, affecting the authority of the United Nations to intervene in the domestic affairs of the members, is contained in Chapter IX, dealing with international economic and social co-operation. Article 56 of this chapter provides that all members pledge themselves to take joint and separate action in co-operation with the organization for the achievement of the purposes set forth in Article 55. This is the article that sets forth the functions of the Economic and Social Council with a view to the creation of the basic conditions deemed necessary for peaceful and friendly relations among the nations. Among these conditions is universal respect for and observance of human rights and fundamental freedoms. This may seem to be no more than a reiteration of the duty to fulfill in good faith the obligations of membership imposed upon the members in Article 2 of the Charter. Article 56, however, adds to the earlier statement of a principle a clear explanation of the procedure to be followed by the members in the fulfillment of this duty. They are specially enjoined to co-operate with the Organization by both joint and separate action for the promotion of respect for fundamental human rights. If the Organization initiates positive action, the members' are clearly bound also to take appropriate action. How far a breach of this obligation would justify a recommendation by the General Assembly for some kind of action or actual intervention by the Security Council is for the future to reveal. Presumably a vigorous and enterprising Organization should be capable of far-reaching efforts to obtain compliance by a recalcitrant member with its duty to respect the rights of its own people or any part of its people. But what form could these efforts take?

The great defect of the Charter, regarded as a frame of international government, is the lack of an adequate process for enforcing its purposes upon individuals. It can proceed only against nations. The ultimate sanction for its authority is war, and war of the most objectionable kind; namely, a war against its own members. Since the primary aim of the United Nations is to save mankind from the scourge of war, this defective solution of the problem of enforcement is highly unsatisfactory. It casts grave doubt upon the practical capacity of the United Nations, unless its powers are strengthened, to translate the declared faith in fundamental human rights into effective works.

There are some other important exceptions to the rule of the Charter against intervention in matters that are essentially within the domestic jurisdiction of member nations. One of these exceptions is supplied by the provisions inserted since the end of World War II in the constitutions of the vanquished states. The military governments established by the occupying powers have been charged with the duty of reconstructing the governments of the defeated peoples on democratic principles. They have been in a position to guide the framers of the new constitutions in these states and to ensure to all the peoples of such states the enjoyment of their basic rights, in so far as this may be accomplished by writing suitable provisions into the new constitutions. The new Japanese constitution,[1] for instance, was established for the express purpose of substituting a government based upon the sovereignty of the people for that which had previously existed by grace of the emperor. Chapter III of this constitution proclaims a list of rights and freedoms deemed suitable by the proper authorities at General MacArthur's headquarters for an essential part of the foundation of Japanese democracy.

This Japanese bill of rights shows plainly the influence of American ideas. All the people, it declares, have the right to work, but nothing is said concerning the means of guaranteeing this right. The right to own property is declared to be inviolable, but property rights are to be defined by law in conformity with the public welfare. The essentials of the American system of free enterprise are expressly safeguarded, but the door is left open for the adoption of socialistic measures, if the prescribed legislative processes are correctly observed. The American military authorities evidently hoped that the new forms and processes of government would contribute to the security of these rights, as in the United States, but they did not rely wholly upon the separation of powers and a system of checks and balances to make these rights secure. They recognized that in a democracy the self-restraint of the sovereign people is the ultimate sanction for the people's rights. The importance of this fundamental truth is attested by the first article in this chapter of the constitution. It provides that the enjoyment of the rights and freedoms, guaranteed to the people, shall be maintained by the eternal vigilance of the people.

There is, of course, no legal obstacle to the enforcement of these provisions of the Japanese constitution during the continuance of the American military occupation. Sometime, however, the occupation must end and Japan will become eligible for membership in the United Nations. If admitted, the question could arise: What would be the status of these constitutional rights under the Charter of the United Nations? Would the abridgment of such rights by a future Japanese government, bent on pursuing an arbitrary or oppressive course of action, produce a situation that the General Assembly might find likely to impair the friendly relations among nations? Would it not be, in such a case, justified in recommending measures for the peaceful adjustment of a situation likely to endanger the maintenance of international peace? The Security Council also, without awaiting recommendations from the General Assembly, might investigate such a dispute; or, without awaiting the development of a dispute, it might investigate a denial of constitutional rights in Japan which, in its opinion, might give rise to a dispute. If the Security Council found that the continuance of the situation was in fact likely to endanger the maintenance of international peace, it could then decide what measures should be taken in accordance with Articles 41 and 42 of the Charter to maintain international peace.

Apparently, therefore, if the Government of the United States should at some future time have reason to believe that the democratic institutions of Japan were in danger of being overthrown by internal force and violence, it could bring the matter to the attention of the appropriate authorities of the United Nations, with a view to intervention by the United Nations in accordance with the provisions of the Charter. Under the new Japanese constitution there is an express renunciation of war. Article 9 states explicitly that war as a sovereign right of the nation is forever renounced as a means of settling disputes between nations. There can be no doubt that a violation of this article of the constitution would create a situation in which the agencies of the United Nations could act with all the authority conferred upon them by the Charter. Presumably a repudiation by a future Japanese government of its obligation to respect the basic human rights and fundamental freedoms of its own people would also create a situation in which the United Nations could assert its right to intervene with all the authority and powers it might find necessary and proper under the circumstances.

Similar provisions have been inserted in the constitutions

of the German states in the American zone of occupation.[2] Presumably such provisions will eventually be inserted also in the constitution of a united Germany itself, if such a constitution should be adopted before the conclusion of a treaty of peace with Germany. If the provisions of the German state constitutions, adopted in 1946, be any guide, the future constitution of Germany will contain a more systematic and comprehensive statement of basic human rights and fundamental freedoms than that of Japan. These state constitutions were drafted by special constitutional assemblies and each contains a long bill of rights, including not only the traditional rights of the individual, as formulated in the American and French revolutions of the eighteenth century, but also the newer economic and social rights which have been stressed in recent years. Moreover, these German state constitutions contain elaborate provisions for the protection of these rights in the courts, and an independent constitutional court is established with a more effective power of judicial veto than was possessed by German courts under any previous German constitution.

To Americans the most novel and interesting feature of this system of securing constitutional rights in these German states is the provision authorizing the constitutional court to pass upon constitutional amendments, which may be proposed in the future, and to disapprove those deemed by it inconsistent with the general principles of the constitution. Another significant innovation is the provision that groups of voters who endeavor to suppress civil liberties shall not be permitted to take part in the elections. The constitutional court is expressly authorized to decide cases involving exclusion of groups of voters from elections. This provision, if contained in the Weimar constitution of the former German Republic, would have enabled the supreme court to have disfranchised the Nazis, when they had made clear their intention to subvert the democratic constitution, if they should have been able under a democratic electoral system to get into power. A similar provision in the constitution of a future German republic would presumably enable the United Nations to intervene if the German supreme court should prove incapable of performing its duty under such a constitution.

Such a provision for disfranchising the enemies of democracy under a democratic constitution may seem an abridgment of one of the basic human rights; namely, freedom of thought and opinion. Hard experience in combating the Fascists and Nazis in their unscrupulous struggles for power has shown the fallacy of this view. If the right to vote were denied only when there was a clear and present danger that the right would be abused to such a degree as to jeopardize the maintenance of the democratic constitution itself, its denial by such a judicial process as is provided by these new German state constitutions would seem to be consistent with the general principles of free government as understood by Americans. The important matter, however, is that under the United Nations Charter any member nation, which should regard the development of a subversive party, like the Nazis, as a threat to friendly relations among nations, could properly bring the matter to the attention of the appropriate agencies of the United Nations, and intervention by the latter would not be precluded by a German claim that such matters were essentially within the domestic jurisdiction of their own government and hence excluded from the United Nations' field of action.

Another exception to the rule that the United Nations should not intervene in matters which are essentially within the domestic jurisdiction of a member state results from certain provisions in the treaties of peace. The Italian peace treaty, for instance, provides in Article 15 that Italy shall take all measures necessary to secure to all persons under Italian jurisdiction, without distinction as to race, sex, language, or religion, the enjoyment of human rights and of fundamental freedoms, including freedom of expression, of press and publication, of religious worship, of political opinion, and of public meeting. Article 17 [2a] of the same treaty, after noting that measures have been taken to dissolve the Fascist organizations in Italy, provides further that the Italian Government shall not permit the resurgence of such organizations, whether political, military, or semimilitary, whose purpose is to deprive the people of their democratic rights. Similar provisions have been inserted in the treaties with the other states that were associated during the war with the Axis powers. These provisions of the peace treaties were designed to remove the protection of civil liberties from the category of domestic matters and to bring it within the province of international action. Even if these states should eventually be admitted to the United Nations, these treaty provisions would remain in force. They would supply a basis for intervention by the United Nations, if necessary, to ensure proper respect for and observance of fundamental human rights.

What may be achieved by the United Nations under the peace treaties with the defeated powers in World War II may be considered in the light of what was accomplished under the peace treaties that followed World War I. The treaties with the vanquished states and also with the new successor states contained provisions designed to protect racial and cultural minorities against discrimination by the governments to which they were subjected. This system of international protection of minorities functioned with more or less success during the years between the two World Wars. There has been much controversy concerning the degree of success that was attained, but it is at least clear that the essential aim of the system was to shield minorities from the danger of oppression by majorities of their own fellow citizens. In general, these minorities belonged to the same nationalities as those of majorities in neighboring states. It was inevitable, therefore, that neighboring states should be interested in the fate of the various minorities. An important exception was formed by the Jewish minorities in these states. There was no neighboring power specially interested in their protection.

The general situation under these treaties for the protection of minorities was a fertile source of quarrels, which were particularly grave when the neighboring states involved were actually contiguous. It is enough now to recall the difference in the plight of Sudeten Germans in Czechoslovakia and of Jews in Poland or Rumania. The system of international protection of minorities gave the League of Nations authority to examine violations of the minorities treaties and thus made it possible to bring these troublesome disputes out of the realm of bilateral discussion and assure some consideration by an international agency. To what extent such international action achieved desirable results was one of the hotly debated questions during the years between the two World Wars.[3]

The experience of the League of Nations in attempting to protect minorities against denial of equal protection under the laws of the states in which they reside established a precedent for the international supervision of human rights within national borders. It also affords a guide against the repetition of obvious errors. The rights to be protected by the United Nations must be clearly expressed. The obligations of the United Nations must be limited to what may reasonably be expected to be within the competence of an international agency. It will also be necessary to determine in advance whether the aim of international action is to permit the autonomous development of cultural groups with a view to the preservation of their traditional cultures, or merely to protect minorities against discrimination during a period of transition to their eventual assimilation.

Under the treaties following World War I the protection of minorities against denial of the equal protection of the laws did not extend to certain kinds of racial discrimination. For instance, it did not prevent discrimination by others than the lawmakers. Neither did it prevent general oppression involving minorities and majorities alike. The protection of national minorities against oppression by reckless majorities of their fellow citizens, however, is a less ambitious undertaking than the protection of the majorities themselves against the abridgment of their constitutional privileges and immunities by arbitrary and oppressive governments which they are powerless to resist. Whatever may be thought of the achievements of the League of Nations in attempting to enforce the rights of minorities under the peace treaties, it is evident that the task before the United Nations presents greater difficulties.

The problem of enforcing respect for and observance of basic human rights in states which are already members of the United Nations presents greater difficulties than that of enforcement in the vanquished states. The United Nations Commission on Human Rights proposes to meet these difficulties by submitting a Covenant for ratification by the member nations. This Covenant is shorter than the proposed Declaration and omits the general principles of government and the good advice which form so large a part of that document. It contains specific limitations upon governmental power, both substantive and procedural. The Commission treats them more precisely than it treated the corresponding provisions in the Declaration, and emphasizes particularly the procedural limitations. The proposed Covenant reflects the dominant influence of Anglo-American legal concepts. In the Declaration the influence of French concepts is more conspicuous. The purpose of the Commission on Human Rights to promote respect for human rights by procuring the incorporation of a body of specific liberties into the laws of the member nations is clearly manifested. The effectiveness of this plan, however, is limited to the particular nations that ratify the proposed Covenant, provided that at least two thirds of those represented in the General Assembly of the United Nations approve the proposal.

American experience with the enforcement of fundamental human rights indicates that this part of the plan of the Commission on Human Rights would be effective in a member state which should ratify the Covenant, provided that it possessed a system of law enforcement like that of the United States. The rights contained in the proposed Covenant are for the most part restatements or amplifications of the traditional American rights sanctified by the federal and state bills of rights. There is no attempt to include the substance of what President Roosevelt called a new economic bill of rights or to guarantee in any way the new freedoms from want and from fear. There are a few additions to the traditional list of civil rights that would require legislative action in order to become fully effective. For example, there is a provision that every person shall have an enforceable right to compensation in respect of an unlawful arrest or deprivation of liberty. A court of law might take judicial notice of this right, if the proposed Covenant were approved by two thirds of the General Assembly and ratified by the Government of the United States, but the unfortunate victim of conviction and imprisonment for a crime that he did not commit would still be dependent upon legislative action for his money, if not for release from prison. The provision that no one shall be convicted or punished for crime except after a public trial might be interpreted to prevent a repetition of such a proceeding as the trial of the Nazi saboteurs during the recent war. The provision that no one shall be required to perform any act which is contrary to his religion is in line with the final action of the Supreme Court in the flag-salute cases. It is now a strictly academic question what the effect of such a provision would have been if the original decision in the Gobitis Case had been allowed to stand. In general, the judges would have no difficulty in giving effect to the provisions of the Covenant under the Constitution of the United States.

An important exception to this view results from the provision that seems to require the enactment of something like the proposed fair-employment practices bills both by Congress and by the state legislatures. The Covenant states expressly that the parties which ratify it recognize certain principles as being among the human rights and fundamental freedoms founded on the general principles of law recognized by civilized nations. It has already been argued before the Supreme Court in a group of cases this winter that the fundamental human rights referred to in the Charter have already become a part of the supreme law of the land and should be enforced in appropriate cases by the courts. This argument was offered in support of a plea that land covenants, discriminating against members of certain races, should be declared invalid under the Charter, since its ratification by the United States has presumably made it a part of the law of the land. Whatever may be the decision of the Supreme Court on this point, it seems clear that such a decision would be necessary in similar cases, if the proposed Covenant should be ratified by the United States. The power of the judges under the American system of law enforcement would give vitality to the fundamental human rights, which might be protected by such a covenant, even if American legislators were reluctant to enact suitable enforcement legislation and executive officers were negligent in the performance of their duties.

American experience with the enforcement of fundamental human rights suggests also that there are serious limitations upon the effectiveness with which universal standards would be enforced by many of the member nations. The provisions of such bills of rights are not self-operative; they have to be applied by men. Their practical application involves their interpretation by political agencies and by courts of law. American experience suggests that, whatever may be the attitude of judges, political agencies at best may be expected to do what is popular and to give fundamental human rights an interpretation that is acceptable to the majority of the people rather than to the minorities who most need their protection. In countries in which there exists what Americans like to call a government of law and not of men, the opinions of judges will weigh heavily in the interpretation of such rights. The great merit of such a system is that citizens' rights will be decided by a body of men whose professional training ensures special competence in such matters and whose security of tenure offers some protection against the shifting currents of political opinion.

There are few countries, however, in which the judges can play so important a part in the protection of basic human rights as in the United States. Even in England, where devotion to the reign of law matches that in the United States, the importance of judicial opinion in the interpretation of basic human rights is considerably less than in the United States. In England, as Professor Laski [4] has well said: "Statutes are not to mean merely what the ministry of the day may be tempted to try to make them mean. The intention of Parliament is to be discovered by a body of independent persons, free from any direct interest in the result, and trained by long years of practice to standards of judgment by which that intention may be tested." Yet Parliament does not have to accept as a precedent for the future a judicial decision that it finds unsatisfactory or displeasing. It can always amend the statute in order to give effect to its own opinion despite the opinion of the judges. In the United States an unpopular decision must be accepted by all concerned, though it need not be allowed to stand as a precedent for the indefinite future. Yet if a constitutional amendment is required to prevent a decision from becoming a precedent, the opinions of the judges are less likely to be overruled by political action than in Great Britain. Judicial review in the American sense is, as Laski put it, "happily unknown to the British Constitution."

The consequence of the inferior influence of judges in those countries that have adopted the English view concerning the nature of a reign of law is greatly to narrow the list of rights regarded even by the judges as basic and fundamental. In the report of the British Committee on Ministers' Powers,[5] published a dozen years ago, there is an interesting discussion of what the authors of the report called "natural" justice. The first and most fundamental principle of it, the report declares, is that a man may not be a judge in his own cause. The second principle is that no party ought to be condemned unheard and that, if his right to be heard is to be a reality, he must know in good time the case that he has to meet. But the learned authors of this report did not insist on any particular procedure by which the party is to be informed of the case he has to meet or by which his own case is to be heard. They were uncertain whether there were additional principles of natural justice, though they mentioned as a possible third principle that a party is entitled to know the reason for the decision. These learned authors were not interested in basic human rights other than procedural rights, and were satisfied with a much more elementary set of procedural rights than would be regarded as essential in the United States.[6] It is unlikely that judges in most parts of the world would be as deeply concerned with the technical aspects of due process of law as in the United States or would as generally deem them essential for a proper observance of fundamental human rights.

In the Soviet Union, as in England, there is insistence on what are regarded as essential procedural rights, but the provisions for the safeguarding of such rights in the Soviet Union would seem as imperfect to Englishmen as the English arrangement must seem to many Americans. Chapter IX of Stalin's constitution of 1936 deals with the courts and the state attorney's office.[7] One article in this chapter provides that in all courts of the Soviet Union cases are to be heard in public, unless otherwise provided by law, and the accused is guaranteed the right of defense. In the English-speaking countries this would seem exceedingly precarious protection for the rights of the individual against abridgment by the acts of public officers. Though there is a so-called right of defense in a Russian criminal prosecution, it seems to amount to no more than a right to a public trial, unless the law-making agencies of the government for reasons satisfactory to themselves authorize a secret trial. The further provision of the constitution of the Soviet Union, that judges are independent and subject only to the law, is deprived of much of its force in the eyes of the English-speaking peoples by the lack of any real security of tenure. Under the constitution the judges are elected by the supreme and local soviets for terms of only three or five years. It does not seem possible that judges can be independent in the American or English sense of the word, when in fact they are so dependent upon the lawmaking agencies for the continuance of their appointments. Yet even these arrangements for the independence of judges and the safeguarding of procedural rights would doubtless seem attractive in some parts of the world.

It is evident that such rights as may be included in the proposed International Covenant, with a view to their incorporation in the fundamental laws of the member states of the United Nations, will be enforced unequally in different parts of the world. The American experience with the effort to secure a uniform interpretation of constitutional rights in all the states of the Union by the independent action of the state governments does not justify the expectation that universal respect for basic human rights will be obtained in a uniform manner among all the different members of the United Nations. Seventy years passed after the adoption of the Fourteenth Amendment before the Supreme Court decided that a Negro was entitled to an opportunity for a university education equal to that enjoyed by a white man.[8] Another ten years passed before it decided that this equality of opportunity should be enjoyed without unreasonable delay.[9] But these were decisions of the federal Supreme Court. There is no way of knowing how long Negroes would have had to wait for an equal opportunity to a university education, if the decision had been left to the supreme courts of the states where discrimination against Negroes was supported by the opinion of the white majorities. American experience points strongly to the conclusion that progress toward uniform and high standards will be exceedingly unequal and in many nations disappointingly slow, unless these rights are brought directly under the protection of international courts of justice, established by the United Nations and surrounded with all the safeguards for the independence of the judges that an international organization can provide.

This negative conclusion calls for further consideration of the outlook for the promotion of respect for fundamental human rights by means of a declaration on human rights such as is proposed by the United Nations Commission on Human Rights. There are three methods of enforcing such an international declaration. The first is that which depends not only ultimately but also immediately upon the eternal vigilance of the several peoples of the United Nations.

The method of enforcement by public opinion in the various member states is dependent for its effectiveness upon the freedom of expression and the development of political thought among their peoples. In the United States, where popular respect for basic human freedoms is supposed to be comparatively wide and deep, recent public-opinion polls have revealed a deplorable ignorance concerning the nature of constitutional rights. It is not surprising, therefore, that the President's Committee on Civil Rights,[10] which published its report early last winter, should have found substantial defects in the actual observance of basic human rights and fundamental freedoms, not only by private individuals and irresponsible groups of persons, but even by public officials charged with the duty of protecting these rights. In other countries, therefore, in many of which the systems of public education, particularly of civic education, are more imperfect than in the United States, less must be expected from the power of public opinion as the means of safeguarding basic human rights. If the content of an international declaration on human rights is determined by a series of compromises between the conflicting opinions of different peoples, as seems inevitable, and if such an international declaration is to be as comprehensive as many ardent advocates of international action believe it should be, it is likely that the measure of enforcement in different countries will be excessively unequal.

In some countries the power of public opinion is reinforced by the activities of the political parties. This is not possible, however, in countries in which the governments operate under the one-party system. A political party that enjoys a monopoly of governmental power cannot be expected to supply a reliable check upon its own measures. In countries in which the multiparty system obtains, there is ample opportunity for the criticism of governmental measures by the members of minority parties, but these minority parties, unless so situated as to form components in coalition governments, are not in a position to make their criticism effective. If the parties that might be disposed to criticize oppressive measures are included within the government coalitions, they are likely to be themselves committed to the support of such measures despite their oppressiveness from the point of view of particular minorities.

The most favorable conditions for the effective expression of opinion by political parties occur under the two-party system. Under such a system, the members of both parties know that, whichever may be in power, the time will come when they will be turned out and the opposition will come in. Whatever precedents may be established by the party in power will stand for the benefit of the opposition when their turn in office comes. All know that, if these precedents seem to sanction arbitrary discrimination against the minority, when the turn of the minority comes the late majority may suffer. Each party knows that it cannot pursue oppressive practices with impunity, for when its tenure of power ends it will be exposed to the same sufferings as it had imposed upon the opposition. Such considerations foster self-restraint in the use of power and promote respect for fundamental freedoms. Under the two-party system, however, minorities not represented by either of the major parties may be excluded from the advantages of the system and, if sufficiently unpopular, may enjoy little protection by the power of what is called public opinion. If there are no effective measures for the protection of personal rights by judicial proceedings, unpopular minorities may in fact be little, if any, better off than all minorities in countries under the one-party system.

The Government of Great Britain offers the best example of what may be done for the protection of civil rights through the activities of an official opposition party. The power of public opinion is effectively utilized by the judicious employment of the question period in the House of Commons. Members of the Government are required to appear in their places and make answer to questions, carefully prepared in advance, usually though not necessarily by members of the Opposition. The members of the Government have due notice of the questions and enjoy the assistance of the permanent officials in preparing their answers. Inadequate replies receive wide publicity in the press and over the radio. Cabinet members, who are responsible for such answers, may not be removed from office by any immediate vote in the House of Commons, but conspicuous ill-success in replying to questions in the House will not only embarrass the Government but also jeopardize the political career of the unfortunate minister. Englishmen set great store by the practical capacity of public opinion, operating through the mechanism of the Opposition party and the question period, to set bounds to the abuse of power by the ministers of the Crown. "The symbol of liberty," Professor Jennings[11] profoundly observes, "is His Majesty's Opposition."

In order to strengthen the power of public opinion, some advocates of an international declaration of rights have recommended the establishment of an international high commission to provide for its enforcement. This commission would be charged with the duty of supervising the observance of human rights among the peoples of the member nations. There are precedents for the establishment of such a commission. For instance, the Permanent Mandates Commission of the League of Nations was charged with the duty of supervising the observance of rights under the Covenant in the mandated territories. The experience of the Permanent Mandates Commission affords some indication of what might be expected from a high commission, if established by the United Nations.

Under the mandate system the League of Nations endeavored to foster respect for and observance of basic human rights in mandated territories in at least five different ways. First, it wrote the guarantees of fundamental freedoms, promised in the Covenant, into the provisions of the mandates. Secondly, it required regular reports from mandatory governments concerning the observance of these rights. Thirdly, it submitted this information to the careful scrutiny of the Mandates Commission. Fourthly, it communicated the findings of this body, together with the comments of the Council and Assembly of the League, not only to the administrative offices of the mandatory powers in the territories, but also to all the states in the League. Fifthly, by publishing these findings, it put them into the hands of the press of all the world.

It was because the Permanent Mandates Commission enjoyed a large measure of public confidence that the mandatory powers, except the Japanese, were reluctant to disregard its opinions. This confidence, one of its ablest members, Professor W. E. Rappard, believed was due not only to the high personal reputation of the commissioners, some of whom were among the foremost authorities on the administration of dependencies, but also to the status of the Commission as an independent expert body. Had it been composed of official representatives, whose respective governments would consequently have been accountable for their published opinions, there is every reason, he has urged, for thinking that the Permanent Mandates Commission would soon have been discredited by the excessive caution required in order to save its members' governments from annoyance and embarrassment. An international high commission on civil rights, constituted like the Mandates Commission, should be able to give effective publicity to the actual observance of human rights in national states, if the demand of the peoples of the world for an international declaration of rights were sufficiently strong to ensure the appointment to the commission of persons of superior character and reputation. However, the enforcement of the provisions of an international declaration of rights by such an agency will always be limited by the nature of public opinion itself, and by its unequal development among the peoples of the different nations under the present circumstances of the world.

The United Nations Trusteeship Council is charged with the responsibility under the Charter for carrying on the work of the League of Nations' Permanent Mandates Commission. It possesses more adequate powers than the Mandates Commission, and should be able to function more effectively. Within the limits of its jurisdiction it should be able to accomplish more than the Mandates Commission to promote respect for the basic human rights and fundamental freedoms of the inhabitants of the trust territories. But only a small portion of the inhabitants of dependent areas live in the trust territories. The Trusteeship Council can make no more than a small dent in the total task of promoting respect for human rights in the modern world.

The proposed International Declaration on Human Rights is as dependent for its practical efficacy upon the state of opinion in the different nations as are the rights to be secured under the proposed International Covenant upon the various national processes of law. Aristotle observed long ago that the essence of any constitution is the system of education. To promote effectively respect for fundamental human rights throughout the countries that have joined the United Nations, it would be necessary to go beyond the mere proclamation of an international declaration of rights. It would be necessary to raise the systems of civic education in many countries to a level where they could meet the standard set by the best systems of civic education. At the present time there is no agreement concerning what systems are best. When Mr. Vyshinsky demanded in the General Assembly of the United Nations that member nations should adopt measures for preventing what he denounced as abuses of the freedom of the press, it became clear that public opinion set a very different standard in the English-speaking countries from what the Soviet Government deemed a suitable standard for international emulation. The standardization of national systems of civic education seems beyond the powers of an international organization based on the principle of the sovereign equality of its members. An international declaration of rights, produced by a series of compromises among the different ideals cherished in different countries, could mean little in the more advanced countries. In the more backward countries it could stand, like the principle of equality in the American Declaration of Independence as expounded by Abraham Lincoln, as a goal toward which their peoples might strive to advance as fast as circumstances should permit. But in the light of the findings concerning respect for human rights in the United States, as reported recently by the President's Committee on Civil Rights, progress toward universal respect for any uniform statement of human rights must be expected to be slow.

There is another possible way of promoting respect for and observance of fundamental human rights, which the Commission on Human Rights has not considered, or at least has not recommended. This is the adoption of a genuine international bill of rights. Such a bill of rights would deal with that part of the general field of human rights which is concerned with the relations between persons in different countries and between such persons and the general international organization itself. It would not be dependent upon enforcement measures in particular states or upon the action of opinion among peoples with radically different traditions and needs. It would be enforceable by direct action through the competent organs of the United Nations. But the enforcement of such an international bill of rights raises the political problem referred to in the first lecture. This problem presents peculiar difficulties and requires special consideration. It will be the subject of the concluding lecture.

Human Rights and the Rights of Nations Under the Charter

THE adoption of the United Nations Charter opened a new chapter in the history of human rights. The high hopes that were aroused by this event were expressed with poetic fervor by one of the American participants in the United Nations Conference on International Organization at San Francisco. "A great beginning," Archibald MacLeish[1] wrote, "a beginning of which Jefferson and Lincoln and the other heroes of the endless struggle for human liberty would have mightily approved!" A more sober estimate of the outlook was expressed by Clark M. Eichelberger,[2] the general secretary of the American Association for the United Nations. "Primarily," he wrote, "the protection of human rights, except in the trusteeship areas, is a matter for the good faith of the nations, the development of public opinion and hard work by the Human Rights Commission." Not all the international lawyers and experts in international relations shared these hopes. Professor Borchard[3] expressed the views of the pessimists with exemplary restraint when he wrote: "Our conclusion must be that, however praiseworthy the objective, the chances that the United Nations will implement their promises and hopes [that is, regarding respect for human rights] by provisions of positive law, and especially that they will enforce these provisions effectively, are rather less than rosy." Professor Nathaniel Peffer[4] was so pessimistic as to doubt whether it was wise for the untried United Nations to undertake so delicate and difficult a problem as the framing of an international bill of rights.

It is too soon to pass judgment upon these various atti-

The Notes to this lecture begin on page 155.

tudes. But it is not too soon to note the promptitude and persistence with which the United Nations has pursued the declared purpose of achieving international co-operation in promoting and encouraging respect for human rights and for fundamental freedoms for all. It is not too soon to recognize the impressive energy and infectious zeal with which the Commission on Human Rights, under the wise and inspiring leadership of Mrs. Franklin D. Roosevelt, has entered upon its task. The work of the Commission and of the Nuclear and Drafting Committees and of the Sub-Commissions on Freedom of Information and of the Press, on Protection of Minorities against Discrimination, and on the Rights of Women attests the resolute determination of the officers of the United Nations to make good the Charter's reaffirmation of faith in fundamental human rights and in the dignity and worth of the human person. This effort has now reached the interesting stage where the opinion of mankind is invited upon specific proposals for an international bill of rights. It is already too late to charge the framers of the Charter with hypocritical pretensions or untimely and unrealistic enterprise.

Experience shows, however, that the obstacles in the way of ungrudging agreement upon the contents of an international bill of rights and of its successful enforcement are formidable. The reason why these obstacles are formidable is plain. Any attempt to establish an international bill of rights as a vital part of the ways of life of the peoples of the world involves a redefinition of the relationship of the individual to the society in which he lives. The dominant political form of contemporary society is the national state, and the national state is highly charged with the dynamic purposes and the powerful sentiments which make the legal fiction of sovereign equality a potent factor in international politics. To try to promote respect for fundamental freedoms by framing an international bill of rights means the beginning of an audacious adventure in the development of the relations not only among individuals, but also between states and the general organization of mankind.

The most cursory inspection of the contents of the proposed International Bill of Rights shows how far-reaching must be the efforts to redefine the relationships of the individual to his particular national state, if this bill of rights is to be effectively implemented. The United States is presumably one of the states that would find the least difficulty in giving practical effect to these rights. The freedoms of speech and expression and of worship, as they might be interpreted and applied by an international court of justice, would not perhaps involve such intimate intervention in the American way of life as the attempt to give effect here to uniform world-wide versions of the freedoms from want and from fear. Yet the recent experience of American politicians with the problem created by the growing demand for equal rights for Negroes and recent judicial experience with the problem created by the propaganda of Jehovah's Witnesses for a reign of the saints suggest that the people of the United States would not readily submit to the readjustment of the relations between saints or Negroes and the rest of our people by the agencies of a general international organization. To impose any but an American version of freedom from want upon the American people would be an even more hazardous undertaking. The American people in their present mood are highly unlikely to submit to any readjustment of the relations between the Communists and the rest of the people by any authority other than their own.

The problem created by an effort to establish a uniform world-wide version of the freedom from fear involves more than a redefinition of the relations between the individual and his national state. It involves a redefinition of his relationship to organized mankind. Under the present Charter of the United Nations this relationship is indirect and remote. But it may be argued—many reasonable persons in fact do argue persuasively—that the organization of mankind is so imperfect as to make this relationship exceedingly unsatisfactory. The existing organization offers little security, for instance, against the danger of such an unannounced and ruinous attack by one major power upon another, as has long been apprehended by the atomic scientists and against the consequences of which they have issued the most earnest warnings. The Commission on Human Rights, however, has no authority to propose improvements in the organization of mankind and under these circumstances can do little to give greater reality to the freedom from fear.

There is doubtless something the Commission on Human Rights might do within its limited authority to secure greater freedom from fear. It might recommend that all members of the United Nations follow the excellent example of the French and the Chinese and include provisions in their written constitutions, if they possess such constitutions, pledging the national faith that they will undertake no war of aggression nor employ their armed forces against the liberty of any people. The constitution of the Fourth French Republic states specifically that on condition of reciprocity France consents to the limitations of sovereignty necessary to the organization and defense of peace; and the new Chinese constitution explicitly provides that the Chinese Republic will support the Charter of the United Nations. Such provisions in the fundamental law of any nation, if duly respected by its people and observed by their government, would modify the relation of the individual to his own national state. Neither the present policy of the French Government with respect to the coercion of the peoples in their Indo-Chinese territories nor the present attitude of the various factions in China toward their new constitution encourage the hope that much can be accomplished in the near future by means of such constitutional limitations, but this is a kind of action that can be promoted by an international commission on human rights. It, at least, does not require the assumption of responsibilities by the United Nations that its organization is not in a position to perform.

Such considerations point toward certain conclusions concerning the proper objectives of an international bill of rights. It is surely necessary to declare clearly that no person anywhere should be deprived of his rights or discriminated against in any way on account of his race, language, or religion. A breach of this basic obligation would give rise to complaints which might be publicly discussed at meetings of the General Assembly or of one of the councils of the United Nations. Appropriate action could then be taken in accordance with the provisions of the Charter. But neither American experience, nor that of the League of Nations between the two World Wars, warrants the expectation that much is to be accomplished by trying to define precisely the local civil rights of persons under the widely differing ways of life which continue to exist in different parts of the modern world. The relationship of the individual to his own state is an intimate matter which for the most part the peoples of different countries wish to adjust in accordance with their own traditions and circumstances. What the United Nations under the present Charter can best do to promote respect for human rights among different peoples with their own peculiar notions and customs is to follow the example of our own people at the time of our Revolution. Something can be accomplished by proclaiming in a solemn state paper the general principles of good government and by setting forth good advice concerning the conduct of public affairs. But detailed descriptions of specific liberties of many different kinds and meticulous regulation of specific legal processes presuppose a degree of uniformity in the ways of life of the various peoples of the modern world that is plainly contrary to fact. The world is not one world in its understanding of the nature of liberty or in its practical application of due process of law.

In the light of experience at home and abroad the position taken by Mrs. Roosevelt in the discussions of the Commission on Human Rights at its recent session seems to be thoroughly sound. She remonstrated against the attempt to expand the proposed International Bill of Rights into a positive statement of desirable solutions for all the problems produced by the principal conflicts of interest among the peoples of modern national states. She herself had proposed a much briefer declaration of rights than that favored by a majority of the Commission. Even her list of rights, comparatively brief as it was, might well be further abbreviated. The most effective international declaration of rights would perhaps be one that attempted to do no more than to give fresh sanction and wider authority to the original Four Freedoms. Such a declaration would possess great inspirational value without committing all the members of the United Nations to uniform solutions of their domestic problems regardless of basic differences in the character and achievement of their respective peoples. It would constitute a standing invitation to all to advance as rapidly as possible toward a universally acceptable goal, but it would not involve the assumption of responsibilities by the United Nations for the adjustment of relations between individuals and their own national governments, which were not assumed in the United States until the time of the Fourteenth Amendment. The peoples of the modern world are far from ready to add anything like the Fourteenth Amendment to the Charter of the United Nations.

There is, however, one clear responsibility in the quest for international co-operation in promoting respect for human rights which the Commission on Human Rights might well undertake. It is a responsibility that has not been discharged in the recent drafts of an international bill of rights. This is the responsibility for defining the relation of the individual to international society as organized under the present Charter of the United Nations. An international bill of rights, which would be fairly comparable with the original American federal Bill of Rights, would deal with that part of the general field of human rights that is concerned with the relations between persons in different countries and between such persons and the general international organization itself. Such a bill of rights would not be dependent upon enforcement measures in particular states or upon the action of opinion among various peoples with radically different traditions and needs. It would be enforceable by direct action through the competent organs of the United Nations.

There is much difference of opinion concerning the feasibility of such a bill of rights. Mr. Cord Meyer, Jr.,[5] president of the United World Federalists, in his thoughtful book, *Peace or Anarchy,* has written that a bill of rights should be added to the Charter, guaranteeing a fair trial to those accused of violating world laws. This bill of rights would be binding only on the United Nations. It would not apply to the operations of national governments and should not be employed, he thinks, to interfere with their domestic affairs. No attempt would be made, according to this view, to extend the protection of an international bill of rights to the world's inhabitants except in their relations to the United Nations.

The contents of such a bill of rights would be more restricted than those of an international declaration of rights, designed to be enforced only by the power of public opinion, or of a covenant to be incorporated into the fundamental laws of national states. Its scope would be defined presumably by the extent of the lawmaking power that might be conferred upon the legislature of a strengthened United Nations. Mr. Meyer expresses the hope that, with the fear of imminent attack removed by an appropriate strengthening of the United Nations, many national governments which do not now feel sufficiently secure to allow civil liberties to their citizens will feel able to do so. Meanwhile, he concludes, all that can be accomplished is to ensure respect for due process of law in cases arising under laws enacted by the United Nations. In short, he advocates an international bill of rights similar to the original American federal Bill of Rights.

The defect in Mr. Meyer's proposal is that the United

Nations Organization does not now possess lawmaking power. The Security Council possesses executive power, but neither this council nor the General Assembly has any authority to legislate on any matter so as to prescribe a rule of behavior for individuals except their own employees. The Organization deals with the governments of states and only through them can regulate the behavior of natural persons. There is, therefore, nothing to which such an international bill of rights as he suggests could apply. A proposal for an international bill of rights, regarded as a means of limiting the legislative authority of the United Nations, is a counsel of perfection. It could raise a standard of good conduct which might serve as an ideal until such time as legislative powers should be granted to the United Nations. Meanwhile, such a proposal is of interest as part of a persuasive plea for the strengthening of the existing institutions of world government.

Mr. Roger N. Baldwin,[6] the head of the American Civil Liberties Union, has given thought to the same subject. His opinion is that there is an important area of human rights involved in the relations among, as well as within, the different nations. Among such rights, according to Mr. Baldwin, are freedom of international communication by radio, cable, news films, and travel, the rights of aliens coming before national courts to suitable protection by the laws, and the right of peoples to have the recognition or nonrecognition of new governments and independent states determined upon sound general principles. These areas, in his opinion, offer a far more productive opportunity for immediate and practical action than the difficult and lengthy efforts required to bring all or any appreciable number of nations to the acceptance in fact, and not merely in words, of a uniform bill of basic human rights. In short, he would define more rationally the relation of the individual, not to his own national state, but to the world society represented by the United Nations.

Mr. Baldwin's proposal is thoroughly realistic. The vast

area of human rights involved in guarantees among, not within, nations is already a source of conflict in international politics. The iron curtain excludes many of the peoples who have joined the United Nations from direct contact with other peoples with whom they would gladly establish friendly relations. In order to secure the blessings of free intercourse and to perpetuate mutual friendship, it is essential that the people of each state should at least be able to communicate freely with one another and to exchange ideas, if not merchandise. Precisely what should be the privileges and immunities of citizens of the United Nations in their personal dealings with one another is not to be determined without careful deliberation. Presumably these privileges and immunities are not exactly the same as those enjoyed by citizens of the United States in their dealings with one another under the present Constitution or even under the earlier Articles of Confederation. But the analogy between the Articles of Confederation, as a scheme for adjusting the relations among citizens of the United States in that stage of the development of the Federal Union, and the Charter of the United Nations in the present stage of the development of an international government for the people of the world is suggestive. A further examination of its implications should cast a helpful light upon the problem of promoting greater respect for fundamental human rights in the modern world.

A beginning has already been made in the redefinition of the rights of the peoples of the world considered as a single body. The General Convention on the Privileges and Immunities of the United Nations is designed to establish the principle that the international organization of mankind itself possesses some rights. This convention, now in process of ratification, has been supplemented by a special agreement between the United States and the United Nations, determining the status of the permanent headquarters on Manhattan Island and regulating the relations between the Secretariat and the local authorities of New York. The

United Nations acquires the right to operate its own short-wave radio station and other communication services, and to provide for the maintenance of order within its own capitol district. No federal, state, or local official may enter the district without the consent of the secretary-general. The local authorities undertake, however, to provide adequate public services, such as water, electricity, and fire protection, and, if required, to supply a sufficient number of police to preserve order within the district. The United Nations, on the other hand, agrees that it will prevent its capitol from becoming a refuge for persons seeking to avoid arrest or legal service under federal, state, or local laws. The general convention, when adopted, will go further and give protection to the members of delegations attached to the United Nations and to journalists and others who may be assigned to report the proceedings of the General Assembly, councils, and other international agencies.

Such conventions and agreements, however, do not secure the rights of individuals, regarded as members of the whole body of people forming the United Nations. Have they not a right to know what is going on at the headquarters of the United Nations, in the General Assembly and councils and other international deliberative organs, and in the Secretariat? Have they not also a right to communicate their own opinions to the Secretariat and to other appropriate United Nations organs? Have they not a right to travel to their capital both for information and to speak for themselves in person? Have they not a right to discuss publicly in their own homes and neighborhoods the problems of the United Nations and the measures which the various organs at headquarters have under consideration? Finally, have they not a right to advocate publicly compliance by the government of their own country with the recommendations of the General Assembly and councils in matters in which they may be concerned?

These are questions calling for answers which the Commission on Human Rights has a special responsibility to try to formulate. The proposed International Bill of Rights appears to offer answers to these questions, but they are buried in the answers which the Commission's proposals offer to the broader questions raised by its International Declaration and its International Covenant. The proposed Declaration is apparently broad enough to cover all the rights suggested above, but there is no provision for its enforcement other than the appeal to the unorganized opinion of mankind. The proposed Covenant is designed to secure the observance of these rights by appropriate action in particular countries, but it can be effective only in those countries whose governments voluntarily ratify the convention and take the necessary action for honoring their obligations. The countries most likely to show disrespect for the rights of persons, regarded as citizens of the United Nations, are the very countries least likely to respond satisfactorily to the stimulus of the proposed International Bill of Rights.

What is most urgently needed is a short, simple bill of international rights that will assert the privileges and immunities necessary and proper for citizens of the United Nations. It is evident that much of the content of the proposed International Bill of Rights is unnecessary and improper for this purpose. It is not necessary, for instance, for the United Nations to organize the struggle for democratic principles of government within the various member nations. It would be highly improper to take responsibility for the extirpation of unorthodox ideologies everywhere in all their forms. Freedom of speech and expression are splendid goals anywhere in the world, but the quest for their attainment in a particular country must be planned in accordance with local circumstances, needs, and previous attainments. Democracy means different things to different peoples. The framers of the American Constitution in 1787 would have resented an attempt by any external authority to impose alien concepts of democracy upon the American people at that time. Many peoples in the modern world are less advanced along the road toward democracy than were the American people in 1787. Each must be free to organize in its own way the struggle for democracy in its own government. We cannot impose our concept of democracy upon the peoples of the Soviet Union. We do not intend to let them impose their concept upon us. The union of peoples in the United Nations cannot function as a single centralized union. It is at best a loose form of federal union.

A suitable bill of international rights will express a more modest purpose than the immediate establishment of universal and uniform regulations for the printing, broadcasting, and other communications industries, to say nothing of the relations between church and state or between different classes of the population in the various countries of the modern world. It will not try to determine for the people of Iceland what privileges, if any, should be extended to the local proletariat in the struggle to materialize the freedom from want, or what privileges should be taken away from the Moslem mullahs in the Imamate of Yemen in the interest of a greater freedom of worship in that country. It certainly ought not to try to impose on all peoples throughout the world precisely that degree of freedom for radio newscasters and commentators which represents the momentary compromise in this country between the interests of the proprietors of broadcasting stations in the development of profitably sponsored programs and the interest of the public in ready access to authentic news and well-considered opinion. Television seems to be destined for a brilliant future, both as a branch of the entertainment industry and as a facility for civic education. We Americans wish the allocation of wave lengths and of time between those who would televise baseball games and prize fights and those who would help us watch our representatives in action at city halls and state capitols to be determined by policies set at Washington rather than at Lake Success.

What is most important for the content of a bill of international rights emerges from the discussions at recent international conferences on the communications industries. The minutes of the United Nations Conference on Freedom of Information at Geneva (March-April 1948) and of the international conferences on civil aviation and on oceanic cables and radiotelegraphy disclose the problems with which a bill of international rights might best deal. There is most urgent need for international agreement to secure the prompt removal, or at least the reduction and eventual removal, of political barriers and economic restrictions that impede the flow of information across national borders. Some of the basic principles of such an agreement were well stated in one of the reports published by the Hutchins Commission on the Freedom of the Press.[7] They include: a guarantee of equality of access to sources of information for all persons in a country, citizens or subjects and aliens alike; the organization of a foreign correspondents' association at all important news centers with a suitable code of ethics and a right of appeal from the orders of local public-relations officers to an appropriate organ of the United Nations; a guarantee that no country will expel an accredited foreign correspondent or interfere with his normal activities, pending appeal to the United Nations; a guarantee that no country will arbitrarily discriminate against foreign publications, radio broadcasts, or motion pictures; and a right of fair sale for books in foreign countries.

In order to implement these international rights the authors of this report proposed the establishment of a special commission under the United Nations Economic and Social Council to promote the free flow of true information across national frontiers and to remove artificial barriers obstructing such a flow. This agency would check the observance of international rights in various countries and publish its findings and recommendations, assist the foreign correspondents' associations in securing respect for their rights at the various news centers, and investigate alleged violations, wherever they might occur. It might also investigate conditions in areas where the distortion of facts and fomenting of international ill will threatened to become a source of international friction, and report to the Economic and Social Council or in case of need to the General Assembly. These are functions that might well be performed by a permanent United Nations Commission on Human Rights, when the present commission has discharged its preliminary task of framing a suitable bill of international rights. Such activities are not only more urgent, but also more appropriate, for an international agency than an attempt to procure compliance in the various countries of the world with the provisions of a standardized bill of rights designed to control the relations between the individual and his own national state in matters not directly affecting his relationship to the other peoples of the modern world.

The obstacles that stand in the way of universal respect for the right of the individual to communicate with the headquarters of the United Nations and with his fellow men in other countries are doubtless great. The greatest perhaps is the suspicion that a general right of international communication would be abused by persons who would be incapable of communicating the truth without prejudice or who would seek to propagate interested views with malicious or even subversive intent. It is clear that no person can be permitted to utilize the facilities of international communication for the purpose of fomenting hatred between nations or subverting the institutions of any nation by incitements to unlawful action and violence. The line between reasonable and seditious propaganda is not easy to draw. The people of the United States had an instructive experience in problems of this kind a century and more ago when the Northern abolitionists were using the mails to disseminate their critical opinions concerning the institution of Negro slavery in the South. The path to the right use of the facilities for international communication is not smooth. But this is the kind of problem to which the advocates of concerted efforts to promote greater respect for human rights throughout the world should address themselves.

The best formula for a bill of international rights was discovered long ago. Immanuel Kant,[3] in his timeless essay on *Eternal Peace,* set forth what he termed the definitive articles of a perpetual peace among states. They were three in number, of which the third is the one containing the formula for a bill of international rights. The rights of men as citizens of the world, Kant suggested, should be restricted to the conditions of universal hospitality. By this he meant the right of a stranger, as long as he conducts himself peacefully, not to be treated as if he were an enemy. Kant did not hold the opinion that the stranger had a right to be entertained like a specially invited guest. But he insisted that all men are entitled to travel about the earth and to make friends, if it should so happen, wherever they go.

Kant was convinced that this was the essential condition for the establishment of friendly relations between separate countries. He was well aware that this had not been the general practice in the relations between peoples who were unacquainted with one another. Peoples, who regarded themselves as civilized, were accustomed to reckon the inhabitants of newly discovered lands as of no account and to treat their countries as if they belonged to nobody. Those whom these peoples deemed barbarians, on the other hand, were apt to assume that strangers were enemies. They even treated the victims of shipwreck as if they had lost their claims to human rights. Kant was able to believe that the considerate treatment of strangers, what we now call the "Good Neighbor" policy, could become in the fullness of time the basis of wholesome international relations under the protection of law.

Kant held the opinion also that the laws of universal hospitality should be founded on a federation of free states. This was the second of his definitive articles on the conditions of perpetual peace. He believed that there was as much reason for forming a union of peoples in order to establish universal laws as for forming the familiar national states in order to establish justice under national laws and secure the other objects of organized states for their particular peoples. He distinguished clearly between a consolidated world state, which he declared to be unnecessary for achieving the purpose of the peoples in reducing to law the terms of universal hospitality, and a federation of national states, which he deemed indispensable for the accomplishment of this limited purpose. He possessed an astonishingly clear understanding of the principle of federalism, considering how recently it had been worked out—when Kant was formulating his ideas on world federation—in the Constitution of the United States.

Kant did not mention the American Constitution, but he perceived the possibilities of the federal principle for the prevention of international wars as correctly as if he had been the recipient of the famous letter written by Franklin to M. Le Grand in France at the close of the Federal Convention. Nor did he imagine anything like a world constitutional convention, for the purpose of framing a world federal constitution. He supposed that any well-ordered federal republic would have the capacity to expand by the acquisition of additional member states, until it should eventually include all the self-governing peoples of the world and be thus sustained by the organized opinion of mankind. We now live in a world in which there are two federal systems, that of the United States and that of the Soviet Union, each of which is theoretically capable of world-wide expansion. A conflict between them for the allegiance of mankind would pose a problem which even the transcendant genius of Kant did not foresee.

Kant's definitive articles of a perpetual peace among states, however, contained a third principle for securing the blessings of universal liberty under a reign of the laws of international hospitality. This principle was expressed in the first of his three articles; namely, that the civil constitution in every state should be republican. Kant's idea of a republic was manifestly inspired by his reading of Rousseau, and his confidence in the eventual attainment of a federal state of peace among men rested upon his faith in the reality of a general will. The subsequent history of republicanism has revealed obstacles to the progress of the republican form of government, not foreseen by Rousseau and Kant, and suggests that the efforts of those who see visions and dream dreams of future happiness for mankind, to be gained by political methods, are apt to be frustrated by the folly and weakness of men and women themselves. The peoples of modern states seem capable of developing a general will, which would make pacific political methods of adjusting world relations a desirable substitute for organized intimidation and international violence, but too often the indispensable general will dissolves in a welter of particular wills, conflicting purposes, and bellicose action.

Kant himself retained to the end a serene confidence that the principle of universal hospitality was the proper basis for the rights of man. His confidence was based upon a theory of progress,[9] which once stimulated sanguine hopes among those who observed the course of events with a reflective eye, but which has now lost much of its creative power in a large part of the modern world. The history of the human race, he was convinced, may be regarded as the gradual realization of a hidden plan of Nature to bring about a perfect political constitution, as the only state in which all the capacities implanted by her in mankind can be fully developed. This proposition seemed to him no more than a logical corollary from two other propositions which he believed he was able to demonstrate. These were that the problem of the establishment of a perfect civil state is dependent upon the problem of the regulation of the external relations between states according to law, and that such an international order was the certain result of the progressive development of the capacities of men by their mutual antagonism in the struggle for existence.

The modern world has incredibly abandoned the belief in progress to the Marxists. Marx unhappily derived his version of the progressive creed from Kant through Hegel, and Hegel's attempt to produce from Kant's theory of progress through social conflict a working guide to political action put too much emphasis on the possibilities of one special kind of conflict, that between the rulers of states and the masses of their populations. Marx transformed the rulers into a ruling class and the possible antagonism between them and their subjects into an inevitable and perennial class struggle. The Marxists' theory of class struggle has served the Communists well in their struggle for power. But it has erected formidable barriers between the republics governed by the Communists and the republics whose peoples are determined to govern themselves without leave from the Communists, and has thereby obscured Kant's grand vision of a pacific world federation founded upon republican principles.

The Communist vision of a world-wide union of soviet socialist republics seems to possess the power to unite diverse peoples over a wide area and to enable them to live at peace with one another. It has accomplished this impressive result in two ways. First, it has given these peoples a general will to regulate their mutual relations by political methods without resort to war against one another. Secondly, it has managed to adjust the relations between the individual and the whole body of people comprising the union without disturbing too much the relationship between the individuals composing each of the various peoples within the union. This is substantial progress, from the viewpoint of the peoples directly concerned, toward the solution of the problem which Kant designated as the greatest practical problem of the human race.

The Communist form of federal republic has appealed most strongly to peoples whose circumstances have seemed to supply the conditions for the particular kind of social conflict assumed by the Marxist dialectic to be normal. Peoples in these circumstances are to be found in many parts of the world. The inhabitants of dependent territories, compelled to submit to the rule of alien conquerors, naturally respond with the greatest alacrity to the incitement of the Marxist theory of progress. Other peoples, separated from their rulers by high social barriers, if not by race, language, or religion, and sharing the common humiliation of gross subjection, easily find the Marxist dogma of social dichotomy plausible and the Marxist road to freedom attractive. In view of the great disparities between the conditions of the rulers and of the ruled in a large part of the world, the Communist solution for the supreme political problem was bound to make headway.

It is evident what response should be made to the Communist challenge by those with a better understanding than the Marxists of the Kantian theory of progress. It consists, first, in adhering steadfastly to the Kantian theory, rightly understood, and proclaiming it to all the world with manifest conviction and genuine fervor. Secondly, it calls for strenuous efforts to build up the middle classes in all countries in order that the antagonism of men in modern society may take the form of conflicts less destructive of the general will than the sharp struggle of a single lower against a single upper class.[10] This is an enterprise with a clearly defined objective which should stir the spirit and stimulate the energies of any strong and generous people. It is an enterprise that, pursued persistently and sagaciously, should bring a rich reward to all the peoples concerned in terms of universal tranquillity.

It is evident also what the function is in such an enterprise of an organized effort to achieve international cooperation in promoting and encouraging respect for human rights and for fundamental freedoms for all without distinctions as to race, sex, language, or religion. An international declaration of rights, broadly conceived and limited to a few simple basic interests to which different peoples can give legal protection in their different ways as their several circumstances make it possible for them to do so, can do much to give a sense of direction and advancement toward the common goal to peoples in different stages of political development. An international covenant, if its sponsors do not overreach themselves by attempting too much with too little preparation, may also contribute to the improvement of legal processes in various countries and thereby ultimately to the greater security of the basic interests of mankind which underlie their dreams of fundamental freedoms. But most important surely is a declaration that shall set forth the rights of international hospitality to the end that men of different countries may meet as friends, not as strangers, and may spread through all lands a better understanding of one another and of the activities of their common agents under the Charter of the United Nations. Respect for the rights of men as citizens of the world to the conditions of universal hospitality would not be long in generating a political power among the peoples of the United Nations, which could transform the present imperfect international organization into a genuine world federation, capable of invaluable services to mankind.

The experience of the United Nations Commission on Human Rights has already demonstrated that there can be no agreement between the Soviet Union and the Western democracies on an international bill of rights defining the relationship of the individual to his own particular state. The concepts of democracy in the Soviet Union and in the West are too radically different to permit such an agreement at the present time. The effort to promote such an agreement is untimely and unwise. It can only put a further strain on the relations between these two parts of the modern world and increase the friction between them. It should not be made by those who seek to create the conditions under which these parts of the world can live together in peace.

A more promising effort under the difficult conditions of the modern world would be directed toward securing the rights of citizens of the United Nations regarded as members of a single world community. If the Government of the Soviet Union sincerely wishes to live at peace with her neighbors in the modern world, such an effort would furnish a convenient opportunity to show its good faith. If, on the other hand, the Soviet Government is determined to recognize the existence of a perpetual state of class war between itself and the nations that reject the dogmas of dialectical materialism and refuse to accept a dictatorship of the proletariat instead of a democratic republic, these nations must continue to strive for the realization of their own vision of a rational world order. A general agreement among these nations concerning the privileges and immunities of world citizenship would create a consciousness of common purpose which would be a tower of strength in any conflict between two worlds. Nevertheless, a universal agreement among all the nations concerning the civil rights of world citizens could be the basis of a durable world peace, sustained by the organized opinion of mankind.

The Fundamental Freedom
of Information

THE proceedings at the United Nations Conference on Freedom of Information, held at Geneva, Switzerland, from March 23 to April 21, 1948, concerned one of the most important of the fundamental freedoms and pointed toward the same conclusions as those drawn in the preceding lectures from the proceedings of the United Nations Commission on Human Rights. This Conference met in pursuance of resolutions adopted by the General Assembly of the United Nations and was attended by representatives of more than fifty of its members together with delegations or observers from several nonmember states. It adopted three conventions, for consideration by the Economic and Social Council and by the General Assembly, two articles, for consideration by the Commission on Human Rights, and forty-three resolutions, for consideration by the governments and peoples of the civilized world. The results of its deliberations demonstrate the wide area of agreement among enlightened representatives of the peoples of the world concerning the nature of a basic human right. At the same time they disclose the grave limitations upon the practical capacity of any general international organization to promote universal respect for, and observance of, human rights and fundamental freedoms.

The call for an international conference on freedom of information was issued by the first General Assembly on December 14, 1946. Freedom of information, the General Assembly declared, was a fundamental human right, "the touchstone of all the freedoms to which the United Nations is consecrated." It implied, the call continued, the right to gather, transmit, and publish news anywhere and everywhere without fetters. It was, therefore, an essential factor in any serious effort to promote the peace of the world. It required, however, in the opinion of the General Assembly, "as an indispensable element" the willingness and capacity to seek the facts without prejudice and to spread knowledge without malicious intent. In other words, if freedom of information is to serve the public interest as well as the private interests of reporters, newspaper publishers, radio broadcasters, motion-picture producers, and other special groups, its privileges must not be abused. International co-operation in promoting respect for such a freedom obviously raises many difficult problems of definition and implementation.

Some of the most serious difficulties were emphasized in the proceedings of the second General Assembly. The problem of warmongering was brought up by the delegates of the Soviet Union, and measures for its prevention were proposed which seemed to the American and other delegations to threaten the imposition of a dangerous governmental censorship over the collection and distribution of news and opinion. Despite strenuous opposition by delegates from a few of the countries where Western concepts of the freedom of the press prevail, the General Assembly resolved on November 3, 1947, to condemn "all forms of propaganda, in whatsoever country conducted, which is either designed or likely to provoke or encourage any threat to the peace, breach of the peace, or act of aggression," and directed that this resolution be communicated to the Conference on Freedom of Information. Not content with this action, the General Assembly went further, and on November 15, 1947, resolved that substantial progress in promoting respect for human rights can only be achieved, "if measures are taken to combat . . . . the publication of false or distorted reports likely to injure friendly relations between States." This resolution also was referred to the Conference on Freedom of Information.

Between the date of the first action by the General Assembly and the actual meeting of the Conference, the high hopes held by the United Nations for constructive action deteriorated rapidly. As the United States delegates to the Conference put it in their official report,* "the world situation worsened, political and economic instability increased, and restrictive tendencies with respect to the free flow of information among peoples became more pronounced." Two years after the end of World War II governmental censorship was reported in half the countries belonging to the United Nations. Restrictions of various kinds impeded international trade in periodicals and films. In the vivid words of the official report of the United States delegates: "The world was gradually being divided into petty principalities of controlled thought."

Discussion at the Conference quickly showed the impossibility of universal agreement upon solutions of its major problems. The delegation of the Soviet Union insisted that the governments of all states should take responsibility for the suppression of warmongering. The American delegates were resolutely opposed to the further extension of governmental censorship, even to prevent propaganda inciting to war and the publication of "false and distorted reports likely to injure friendly relations between states." Other influential delegations took an intermediate position, wishing to discourage warmongering, but unwilling to jeopardize unduly the system of free enterprise in the collection and distribution of information. The result was that, in the words of the American delegation's official report, "the search to find common ground in matters of basic principle between the world of freedom and the world of state control was soon abandoned."

The American delegation had its way in framing the leading resolution relating to general principles. A large majority of the delegations agreed that freedom of informa-

---

* United Nations Conference on Freedom of Information, Report of the United States Delegates with Related Documents (Washington, D.C.: Department of State, Publication 3150, 1948).

tion is a fundamental right, not of governments alone, but of the peoples of the world. There was similar agreement that, in order to implement the right of the peoples of the world to be fully informed, the right to gather, transmit, and disseminate news anywhere "without fetters" should be guaranteed everywhere. There was such agreement also that there is a moral obligation on the part of the press and other agencies of information to seek the truth without prejudice and to report the facts without malicious intent, but that this moral obligation should not be enforced by any process of law. The Soviet bloc, however, consisting of six delegations, voted against these propositions.

The American delegation nevertheless was forced to yield to the delegations from other Western countries in the action taken by the Conference concerning propaganda inciting to war and false reporting. British and other important delegations insisted that the Conference should discountenance warmongering in pursuance of the wishes of a majority of the members of the United Nations, as expressed at the second General Assembly, and the American delegation sponsored an acceptable antiwarmongering resolution rather than permit the Conference to consider a more objectionable resolution sponsored by the Soviet delegation. This resolution, the American delegates reported, "became sufficiently ambiguous to permit varying interpretations, without however compromising the American position against government control of the political reporting and expression by news media." The final product of this parliamentary maneuvering was a compromise adopted unanimously by the Conference. Much importance cannot be attached to the text of this resolution, since, as the American delegates confessed, "Soviet propaganda will no doubt revert, nevertheless, to its original contention that governmental suppression is needed to prevent 'propaganda inciting to war.' "

The American delegation was also forced to recognize that the free-enterprise system alone is not enough to assure a satisfactory freedom of information in the modern world.

The Fundamental Freedom of Information

One of the most interesting of the general resolutions adopted by the Conference related to attempts to remedy deficiencies in the supply of the physical facilities for mass communication in the war-devastated and underdeveloped countries of the world. The flow of information among peoples cannot be really free without radio equipment, film projectors, and printing presses. A free press cannot thrive without newsprint. UNESCO had recently found that many thousands of additional tons of newsprint were needed to relieve the most critical deficiencies in these countries. Genuine freedom of information, it was clear, was impossible while such shortages of newsprint continued. The Conference recommended that governments give their support to the UNESCO plan for aid to these countries and invited UNESCO to try to help other countries suffering from an acute shortage of newsprint. American experience suggests that such aid is not likely to be very helpful, unless important governments, including the American, adopt measures no less effective than those taken by the War Production Board during World War II. But such measures in time of peace would involve far-reaching exceptions to the American free-enterprise system and lend unintended encouragement to the Soviet version of freedom of the press.

Though the action of the Conference upon the general principles of freedom of information left much to be desired, its forty-three resolutions undoubtedly contain a great deal of good advice for the peoples of the world. Several of the resolutions recommend useful measures to facilitate the gathering and international transmission of information, such as measures for the better identification of foreign correspondents, for their protection against arbitrary expulsion from foreign countries, and for the mitigation of the hardships of inconsiderate censorship. Other resolutions recommend measures concerning the free publication and reception of information, designed to prevent discrimination and monopoly in the news services of different countries, to standardize the laws regarding libel, and to promote higher ethical standards in the practice of journalism. The Conference gave some attention also to the machinery for promoting the free flow of information, recommending particularly the generous support of the Economic and Social Council's Sub-Commission on Freedom of Information and the Press. This advice should be helpful in removing barriers to the freer flow of information among peoples in the nontotalitarian countries.

The Conference was less successful in its effort to assist the Commission on Human Rights in drafting its proposed International Bill of Rights. It prepared an article on the right to freedom of thought and expression for the Draft Declaration on Human Rights, but the Soviet bloc refused its consent. It prepared an article on the same subject for the Draft Covenant on Human Rights, to which both the Soviet bloc and the American delegation were opposed. The former was a general statement to the effect that everyone should have such a right, including freedom to hold opinions without interference and to seek, receive, and impart information and ideas by any means and regardless of frontiers. This right was not to be enforced by any legal process and would be dependent for its practical effect upon such support as it might obtain from public opinion in the various countries of the world.

The article prepared for the Draft Covenant on Human Rights was more ambitious. In addition to a legal definition of freedom of thought and expression, it contained a list of specific limitations on this freedom, which might legitimately be imposed by governments of the states, which should eventually subscribe to the Covenant, if they wished to do so. Among these specific limitations on the proposed freedom of thought and expression were (1) matters that must remain secret in the interest of national safety, (2) expressions that incite persons to alter by violence the system of government or that promote disorder, and (3) the systematic diffusion of deliberately false or distorted reports that undermine friendly relations among peoples or states. Most of the delegations believed that such an enumeration of exceptions was consistent with the actual practice in democratic countries and would constitute a desirable guarantee against arbitrary restrictive measures, since they would be the only restrictions permitted by international law. Almost all the delegations from the democratic states voted for the draft article in this form.

The American delegation was strongly opposed to specific limitations of this kind in the Draft Covenant. It believed that it was not desirable to try to specify all the limitations that democratic governments now impose on freedom of information or that they might in the future find expedient. It was particularly opposed to the provision relating to the diffusion of false or distorted reports. Such a provision, it feared, could be used as a pretext by arbitrary governments for curbing the dissemination of unfavorable but legitimate information. It preferred to express the right to freedom of information in none but general terms. Hence the American delegation joined the Soviet bloc in opposing this decision of the Conference. This antagonistic attitude on the part of these two important powers raised serious doubts concerning the feasibility of any early agreement by the United Nations upon a Covenant on Human Rights such as had been planned by a majority of the Commission on Human Rights.

The most important action of the Conference was the drafting of three conventions, relating to freedom of information, for consideration by the Economic and Social Council and ultimately by the General Assembly. One of these, proposed by the American delegation, related to the gathering and international transmission of news. The second, proposed by the French, was designed to provide for an international right of correction. The third, proposed by the British, was a more detailed elaboration of the general statement concerning freedom of information contained in the article prepared for use by the Commission on Human Rights in its Draft Covenant. These conventions, if approved by the General Assembly, will be open for ratification by members of the United Nations and will be effective among the ratifying states.

The Draft Convention on the Gathering and International Transmission of News was proposed by the American delegation for the purpose of implementing the general statement of principle which it had persuaded the Conference to adopt. This convention undertook to deal only with the problems of the foreign correspondents—a body of but a few thousand persons—yet indirectly it would affect profoundly the peoples of the world. The articles of this proposed convention were designed to encourage the freest possible movement of foreign correspondents; to protect them against arbitrary expulsion by foreign governments; to give them the widest possible access to news; and to ensure equitable treatment of their despatches. It declared that there are no valid grounds for censorship of international news except in cases relating directly to military security. It sought to regulate in the interest of fairness the operations of military censors. Its adoption by the General Assembly and ratification by the states of the world would mark a long step forward in the relations among their peoples. The opposition of the Soviet bloc, however, forbids the expectation that this step will be universal in the near future.

The Draft Convention, proposed by the French, was designed to provide for the cases where the government of a state feels that a report, sent out by a foreign correspondent, is false or distorted and is likely to injure its relations with other governments. The complaining government would be authorized in such a case to send its own version of the facts to the government of the state in which the report had been published. The latter would then be obliged to make this version available to the information agencies which supply news to the public in that state. These agencies would not be required, however, to publish the correction, though of course the hope of the sponsors of this proposal was that they would ordinarily do so. The French delegation originally proposed to establish machinery under the United Nations for giving due publicity to such official corrections, but this part of its proposal was not adopted by the Conference. The American delegation regarded an attempt to force the publication of corrections of false reports as inconsistent with the free-enterprise system, but pointed out that American newspapers generally follow the practice of publishing necessary corrections of their news reports. The value of this Draft Convention was increased by a provision that the Secretary-General of the United Nations could give publicity to an official correction in cases where the government of the offending state failed to do so.

The Draft Convention, proposed by the British, raised the same problems of policy as the article on freedom of information prepared for use by the Commission on Human Rights in its Draft Covenant. Most of the delegations, representing states in which Western ideas of freedom prevail, supported it strongly, since it confirmed the kinds of limitations on freedom of speech and expression already embodied in their domestic legislation and sanctioned by public opinion among their peoples. The Soviet delegations opposed it, of course, because it would deprive governments in totalitarian states of their complete control over the publication of news and the expression of opinion. The American delegation opposed it, because it would encourage a greater degree of governmental control over the flow of information than seemed consistent with the American system of free enterprise in the communication industries. It actually received in the Conference a greater number of affirmative votes than the American proposal relating to the gathering and international transmission of news. But the opposition of both the American and the Soviet delegations made its future seem less promising.

The proceedings at the Conference on Freedom of Information, like those in the Commission on Human Rights, cast grave doubt on all proposals that seek to promote universal respect for and observance of human rights by regulating the relations between the peoples of individual states and their own governments to a greater extent than is necessary for the purpose of securing greater freedom in the relations between different peoples or between persons in different countries and the government of the international community known as the United Nations. The freedom of information is surely, as the first General Assembly declared, the touchstone of all the freedoms to which the United Nations is consecrated, and must cover the right to gather, transmit, and publish news anywhere and everywhere without fetters, subject to such limitations as may be necessary to prevent its abuse. To secure this right is the first step in securing all the blessings of that general good-neighbor policy which Kant rightly regarded as the essential basis of any serious effort to promote the progress and peace of the world. The proposed conventions, sponsored by the American and French delegations at the Conference on Freedom of Information, point in the direction in which the Commission on Human Rights should strive for further advances. At the present stage in the development of a world federation of free peoples it is the rights of persons as citizens of the international community known as the United Nations, not their rights as citizens of particular states, that require most urgently the protection of international covenants and can be sustained most effectively by the organized opinion of mankind.

The Conference on Freedom of Information made a solid contribution to the development of an alert and sound world opinion. The measures which it proposed for the greater security of international news correspondents form an indispensable part of the rights of persons as citizens of the United Nations. Those proposed for protection against false or distorted reports, likely to injure friendly relations among states, should strengthen the foundations upon which world opinion must rest. But it was a mistake to abandon so soon the search for common ground in matters of basic principle between what the American delegates called in their report "the world of freedom" and "the world of state control." The American admission that a free press cannot thrive without newsprint and the Soviet acceptance of a resolution stressing moral responsibility rather than governmental controls as a partial solution of the problem of warmongering suggest the existence of common ground broad enough to support some necessary agreements concerning the relations of persons everywhere to the organized international community. If the Soviet Government will not now acknowledge the existence of a fundamental freedom to gather and transmit news of all kinds everywhere, greater effort should be made to procure universal recognition of the more limited but more urgent right of persons everywhere to know at least what goes on at Lake Success and to express opinions concerning proceedings there.

Those who believe that the key to better international relations is greater respect for the principle of universal hospitality should concentrate their energies on the struggle to secure first the freedoms which are most immediately essential. In seeking to promote the progress and peace of the world the best should not be permitted to become the enemy of the good. The Commission on Human Rights would serve mankind well by drafting a Covenant on Human Rights that would leave to the governments of the states directly concerned the rights of Americans, Englishmen, Frenchmen, Russians, Chinese, and others, and would strive to secure first the rights of men as citizens of the organized world.

NOTES TO FIRST LECTURE

[1] Standard Oil Company of New Jersey, *Annual Report for 1946*, p. 3.

[2] *Congressional Record*, Vol. 90, Part I, p. 57.

[3] Hersh Lauterpacht, *An International Bill of the Rights of Man* (New York: Columbia University Press, 1945), p. 3.

[4] *Ibid.*, p. 15.

[5] *Annals of the American Academy of Political and Social Science*, CCXLIII (January 1946), 18-26.

[6] *International Conciliation* (New York: Carnegie Endowment for International Peace, December 1946), No. 426, 562-64.

NOTES TO SECOND LECTURE

[1] Georg Jellinek, *The Declaration of the Rights of Man and of Citizens; A Contribution to Modern Constitutional History.* Translated from the German by Max Farrand (New York: Henry Holt and Company, 1901).

[2] William and Mary, sess. 2, c. 2. Cf. George Macaulay Trevelyan, *The English Revolution 1688-1689* (New York: Henry Holt and Company, 1939), pp. 161-63.

[3] Carl L. Becker, *The Declaration of Independence, A Study in the History of Political Ideas* (rev. ed.; New York: P. Smith, 1933), pp. 240-49.

[4] Abraham Lincoln, *Speeches and Letters of Abraham Lincoln, 1832-1865* (Everyman's Library ed.; New York: E. P. Dutton and Company, 1907), speech delivered at Springfield, Illinois, June 26, 1857.

[5] Francis N. Thorpe, comp. and ed., *The Federal and State Constitutions, Colonial Charters, and Other Organic Laws of the States, Territories, and Colonies Now or Heretofore Forming the United States of America* (Washington, D.C.: Government Printing Office, 1909), VII, 3812-14.

[6] *Documents Illustrative of the Formation of the Union of the American States,* 69th Congress, 1st Session, House Document No. 398, p. 716.

[7] *Ibid.*, pp. 1018-20.

[8] *Ibid.*, pp. 1027-44.

[9] Carl Van Doren, *The Great Rehearsal* (New York: The Viking Press, 1948), chap. XIII.

Notes

[10] Madison's letter to Jefferson, October 17, 1788, in Gaillard Hunt, ed., *The Writings of James Madison* (New York: G. P. Putnam's Sons, 1904), V, 269-75.

[11] Jefferson's letter to Madison, March 15, 1789, in Albert Bergh, ed., *The Writings of Thomas Jefferson* (Washington, D.C.: Thomas Jefferson Memorial Association of the United States, 1907), VII, 309-15.

[12] There are many editions of *The Federalist*. The latest is Charles A. Beard, *The Enduring Federalist* (Garden City, N.Y.: Doubleday and Company, 1948).

[13] *Barron* v. *Baltimore,* 7 Peters 243 (1833).

[14] *Dred Scott* v. *Sandford,* 19 Howard 393 (1857). Taney's opinion extends from pp. 399-454; Curtis' opinion, from pp. 564-633.

[15] The Articles of Confederation, Article 4; see Van Doren, *The Great Rehearsal,* Appendix I.

NOTES TO THIRD LECTURE

[1] *The Public Opinion Quarterly,* IX (Fall 1945), 370.

[2] *Ibid.,* X (Summer 1946), 248.

[3] *Ibid.,* X (Fall 1946), 409.

[4] *Ibid.,* X (Winter 1946-1947), 604.

[5] *Fortune,* XXXVI (October 1947), 5-7.

[5a] *Shelley* v. *Kraemer,* 68 S. Ct. 836 (1948).

[6] Thomas M. Cooley, *A Treatise on the Constitutional Limitations which rest upon the Legislative Power of the States of the American Union* (Boston: Little, Brown and Company, 1868). See particularly chap. VII, "The Circumstances under which a Legislative Act may be Declared Unconstitutional."

[7] *Luther* v. *Borden,* 7 Howard 1 (1849).

[8] *Dred Scott* v. *Sandford,* 19 Howard 393 (1857).

[9] *Schwimmer* v. *United States,* 279 U. S. 644 (1929).

[10] *Macintosh* v. *United States,* 283 U. S. 605 (1931).

[11] *Girouard* v. *United States,* 66 S. Ct. 826 (1946).

[12] *Crandall* v. *Nevada,* 6 Wallace 35 (1868).

[13] The Slaughter House Cases, 16 Wallace 36 (1873).

[14] *Hague* v. *C. I. O.,* 307 U. S. 496 (1939).

[15] *Edwards* v. *California,* 314 U. S. 160 (1941).

[16] *Adamson* v. *California,* 67 S. Ct. 1672 (1947). Cf., *In re Oliver,* 68 S. Ct. 499 (1948).

[17] *Fletcher* v. *Peck,* 6 Cranch 87 (1810).

[18] *United States* v. *Lovett,* 66 S. Ct. 1073 (1946).

[19] *Butts* v. *Merchants and Miners Transportation Co.,* 230 U. S. 126 (1913).

17

[20] *Morgan* v. *Virginia,* 66 S. Ct. 1040 (1946).

[21] *Chambers* v. *Florida,* 309 U. S. 227 (1940).

[22] *Lochner* v. *New York,* 198 U. S. 45 (1905).

[23] *Adkins* v. *Children's Hospital,* 261 U. S. 525 (1923). *Morehead* v. *Tipaldo,* 298 U. S. 587 (1936).

[24] *Near* v. *Minnesota,* 283 U. S. 697 (1931).

[25] *DeJonge* v. *Oregon,* 299 U. S. 353 (1937).

[26] *Cantwell* v. *Connecticut,* 310 U. S. 296 (1940).

[27] *Minersville School District* v. *Gobitis,* 310 U. S. 586 (1940). *State of West Virginia Board of Education* v. *Barnette,* 319 U. S. 624 (1943).

[28] *Cox* v. *United States,* 68 S. Ct. 115 (1947). See especially the dissenting opinions of Justices Douglas and Murphy.

[29] Commission on Freedom of the Press, Report (Chicago: The University of Chicago Press, 1947), *passim.* Cf. Morris L. Ernst, *The First Freedom* (New York: The Macmillan Company, 1946).

[30] *To Secure These Rights* (Washington, D.C.: Government Printing Office, 1947). Cf. President Truman's message to Congress, February 2, 1948, 94 *Congressional Record* 960 (House Document No. 516).

NOTES TO FOURTH LECTURE

[1] William H. Beveridge, *Full Employment in a Free Society* (London: G. Allen and Unwin, Ltd., 1944), p. 21.

[2] *Wolff Packing Co.* v. *Industrial Court,* 262 U. S. 522 (1923). See also *Tyson* v. *Banton,* 273 U. S. 418 (1927); *Ribnik* v. *McBride,* 277 U. S. 350 (1928); *New State Ice Co.* v. *Liebmann,* 285 U. S. 262 (1932).

[3] See especially *Nebbia* v. *New York,* 291 U. S. 502 (1934); *Olsen* v. *Nebraska,* 313 U. S. 236 (1941).

[4] See especially the following Jehovah's Witnesses cases: *Martin* v. *Struthers,* 319 U. S. 141 (1943); *Murdock* v. *Pennsylvania,* 319 U. S. 105 (1943); *Follett* v. *McCormick,* 321 U. S. 573 (1944).

[5] *Meyer* v. *Nebraska,* 262 U. S. 390 (1923). *Pierce* v. *Society of Sisters,* 268 U. S. 510 (1925).

[6] *Everson* v. *Board of Education of Ewing Township,* 330 U. S. 1 (1947). *McCollum* v. *Champaign Board of Education,* decided March 8, 1948. The four opinions were by Justice Black, with whom Justices Douglas and Murphy and Chief Justice Vinson concurred; by Justice Frankfurter, with whom Justices Jackson, Rutledge, and Burton concurred; and by Justice Jackson for

himself alone; together with a dissenting opinion by Justice Reed.

[7] As reported in the *New York Herald Tribune,* September 20, 1947.

NOTES TO FIFTH LECTURE

[1] *Japanese Official Gazette,* November 3, 1946. See D. D. Rowe, "The New Japanese Constitution," *Far Eastern Survey,* XVI (January 29, 1947), 13-17; XVI (February 12, 1947), 30-34.

[2] Office of Military Government (United States), Constitutions of Bavaria, Hesse, Wuettenbarg-Baden, Berlin, 1947.

[2a] Cf. Article 49 of the new Italian constitution, effective January 1, 1948, which seems to outlaw political parties employing other than democratic methods in the struggle for power.

[3] See Pablo de Azcárate, *The League of Nations and National Minorities: An Experiment* (New York: Carnegie Endowment for International Peace, 1945).

[4] Harold J. Laski, *Parliamentary Government in England* (New York: The Viking Press, 1938), p. 303.

[5] The Committee on Ministers' Powers Report. Cmd. 4060, 1932, p. 75.

[6] English judges, for instance, were not disturbed by the celebrated 18B Defense General Regulations, 1939; American judges might have discovered the compatibility of these regulations with American principles of due process of law.

[7] See especially Articles 111 and 112.

[8] *Gaines* v. *Canada,* 305 U. S. 337 (1938).

[9] *Sipuel* v. *Board of Regents of the University of Oklahoma,* 68 S. Ct. 299 (1948).

[10] *To Secure These Rights,* chap. II, "The Record: Short of the Goal," pp. 20-29. See also pp. 133-34. For American experience in another field, see John Lord O'Brian, "Loyalty Tests and Guilt by Association," *Harvard Law Review,* LXI (April 1948), 592-611.

[11] W. Ivor Jennings, *The British Constitution* (Cambridge, England: The University Press, 1941), p. 226.

NOTES TO SIXTH LECTURE

[1] The American Jewish Committee, *A World Charter for Human Rights* (New York: The Committee, 1945).

[2] Clark M. Eichelberger, *The United Nations Charter; What Was Done at San Francisco* (New York: American Association for the United Nations, Inc., Commission to Study the Organization of Peace, 1945), p. 20.

[3] *Annals of the American Academy of Political and Social Science,* CCXLIII (January 1947), 117.

[4] *Commentary,* I (January 1946), 58.

[5] Cord Meyer, Jr., *Peace or Anarchy* (Boston: Little, Brown and Company, 1947), pp. 168-69.

[6] Roger N. Baldwin, "International Agreements Can Protect Specific Rights," *Annals of the American Academy of Political and Social Science,* CCXLIII (January 1946), 134-38.

[7] Llewellyn White and Robert D. Leigh, *Peoples Speaking to Peoples; A Report on International Mass Communication from the Commission on Freedom of the Press* (Chicago: The University of Chicago Press, 1946), p. 122.

[8] Immanuel Kant, *Eternal Peace, A Philosophic Essay,* 1795, many editions. See also Carl J. Friedrich, *Inevitable Peace* (Cambridge: Harvard University Press, 1948).

[9] Immanuel Kant, *The Natural Principle of the Political Order,* 1784. Cf. World Peace Foundation edition, *Eternal Peace, and Other International Essays, by Immanuel Kant,* Boston, 1914.

[10] The role of the middle classes in modern states is a subject I have discussed at greater length in my book, *The Middle Classes in American Politics* (Cambridge: Harvard University Press, 1940), Parts I and II, chap. 4.

Index

Index

Index

OTHER PUBLICATIONS—STOKES FOUNDATION

James Stokes Lectureship on Politics
Anson G. Phelps Lectureship on Early American History

NEW YORK UNIVERSITY